Relations*lips*

Relationslips

Life Together in a Falling-Apart World

JASON DRAPEAU

RESOURCE *Publications* · Eugene, Oregon

RELATIONSLIPS
Life Together in a Falling-Apart World

Resource Publications
An Imprint of Wipf and Stock Publishers
199 W. 8th Ave., Suite 3
Eugene, OR 97401

www.wipfandstock.com

PAPERBACK ISBN: 978-1-7252-7752-6
HARDCOVER ISBN: 978-1-7252-7751-9
EBOOK ISBN: 978-1-7252-7753-3

Manufactured in the U.S.A.   07/22/20

Contents

Preface

WARNING: THIS BOOK IS not for the faint of heart. It is not for those who have frail convictions. It is not for those who suppose that the most joyful and abundant life is the way you have always lived it. This book is for those who realize that sometimes life together can be hard, and who are on a mission for this together-life to be vibrant and full of joy.

Many people—even, and sometimes especially, those who follow God and know his Word, the Bible—are unfortunately often terribly inept at carrying on good relationships with others. Disagreements, sour looks, miscommunication, pent-up emotions, back-talk, gossip, tactless Facebook posts, lack of knowledge of God's desires (by even *seasoned* saints), and hundreds of other things have led the masses to general impotence when it comes to basic fundamental fruits of faith such as love, forgiveness, and reconciling to make broken relationships right. And as most people who have read thus far, thinking to yourself "Well, that's clearly not me!" is absolutely an incorrect and ignorant response.

Be forewarned: this book *is indeed* about you . . . it's about all of us. But it is written to help us. It is written to guide us in being the best family members, friends, and followers of Jesus that we can be. Because no matter how well we try to walk in our journeys in life, or no matter in which direction we try to go, we can't escape the fact that life was meant to be spent together, even in a falling-apart world.

If you have picked up this book for the purpose of justifying the reasons that you have broken and fractured relationships, then I'm afraid you will find nothing here that will defend your positions. Rather, you will be faced with conviction, and a challenge to change fundamentally who you are and how you act toward others, in order to be more like God who acts kindly and mercifully toward you.

If you are reading because you are interested in how to make your relationships better and are hoping that the contents of this book will magically materialize the best friendships on earth, then again, I am sorry to disappoint you. "You can lead a horse to water," as the saying goes, but you personally cannot *make* friends, family members, significant others, co-workers, and strangers think that you are the greatest thing on earth since sliced bread. (The biggest reason for this is, of course, because you are *not* the greatest thing on earth since sliced bread. I hate to burst your bubble . . . and I hope you will continue reading on!)

In reading this book, however, you will see God's plan for relationships. His plan is wise, good, and challenging, but it is the only way that you will have fullness of satisfaction and unextinguishable joy in how you relate and feel toward one another. It takes two people to be together in relationships: you, and someone else who is with you. And if one-half of the people who are in every relationship you have with others (that "one-half" being *you*) is filled with joy in following God's relationship plan, then maybe—just maybe—your relationships will improve, and so will your own personal joy as well.

That is my hope. That is my prayer. That is why I have written this book.

So, come and read . . . your life together with others might never be the same.

Acknowledgments

THIS BOOK COMES AS a result of the incredible journey that I have been blessed to take with a number of phenomenal people:

> ‣ The wonderful faith family of Winchester Community Church in West Seneca, NY, who have been patient with my pastoring, encouraging with my preaching, supportive of my writing, and unifying with my passion to radically pursue God's good Word. May we all *always* live out the "Relationship Revolution."

> ‣ My delightful children, who have had to bear with a dad who both overjoys and probably annoys them, because he makes them reconcile with each other when they begin to be frustrated with one another. May you always forgive me when I sin against you, may you always show me grace when I confess my failings before you, may you always forgive and love others regardless of what they say and do to you, and may you continue to live and love like Jesus loves—for he unceasingly loves you.

> ‣ My beautiful wife, who has supported and encouraged me in ministry and in my passions. Your heart for God's mercy and Christ's compassion shows that you exquisitely emulate the truths of this book. May your joy and love continue to fuel mine.

Chapter 1

$$\int$$

The Need for a Revolution

RELATIONSHIPS: NO MATTER THE context—whether in a family, or at work; whether neighbors or strangers; whether close or far apart; whether in the church or somewhere else, life together is just hard sometimes. There are some people that you can't stand, and some people that can't stand you. There are some people who are hard for you to love, and there are some people who just don't love you. There are some people who are difficult to get along with, and there are some people who have a difficult time getting along with you.

Do you ever wonder why sometimes keeping good relationships is hard? I mean, since the entire universe revolves around *you*, if everyone just did things exactly the way you want them to be, then you wouldn't have a problem with anybody! You might have thought, lived, or even said something like the following about others:

> ➤ "I'd be such a better husband if it weren't for my wife."
>
> ➤ "I'd be such a better wife if it weren't for my husband."
>
> ➤ "I'd be such a better parent if it weren't for my kids."
>
> ➤ "I'd be such a better friend if it weren't for everyone who annoys me all the time."

But the bottom line is that our relationships don't work in this manner. You see, the world doesn't revolve around you, or me—nor should it, by the way. And not everyone does things exactly the way you or I want them to be—nor should they, by the way. Whether or not you are the sharpest tool in the shed, you happen to be in the shed with other tools as well. And whether or not you are the strongest tree in the forest, God put you in the forest with other trees. So here we are, firmly planted, strong as steel, living life with others in relationships . . . or relations*l*ips.

I wish that stating the case for a revolution of right relationships was difficult in a book such as this one. Unfortunately, this is not so. We don't have to look very far in order to see fractured and broken relationships around us, and the desperate need to make these broken relationships right:

> ‣ Friends who were once close in heart, and who now wish the other got lost and was a thousand miles away.

> ‣ Estranged family members who are related by blood, but are foreigners in every other facet of life.

> ‣ Co-workers who tolerate each other simply because money in their paycheck is involved, when in reality they wouldn't be caught dead in the same building as each other anywhere else in town.

There are casualties from the relationship battlefield all around us that provide evidence of the fact that life together is difficult, and we aren't living it very well. If not for a revolution—a "revolving" or "turning back" to the way God has planned for life to be lived together (which the Bible calls "repentance")—then not only will our relationships not progress in health, they will actually slip or *regress* in deeper distance and greater sorrow.

Thus far in this book, I have mentioned that God has a plan for life as it is to be lived together. Within the pages that follow, I will be presenting some specifics regarding God's picture-perfect plan for relationships as seen in the Bible—God's Word. Even though I will be gladly and unashamedly turning to God's insights regarding life together, it is not necessary for all readers here to agree with the source of my understanding of right relationships. Regardless of your spiritual background or faith journey, much can be gleaned from this study and observation all the while. In the same way that I can be impressed with a painting in a museum without needing to know who the artist is, or without holding a college degree in Art History, so likewise anyone can be impressed with God's radical and revolutionary plan for how we are to act and react with one another, whether or not you consider yourself a person of strong faith or biblical conviction.

Similarly, whether or not a person acknowledges God, they still may object to the things of God and consequently will also see the outcome of broken relationships due to failing to embrace God's guidance on the subject. Whether or not a person reads the Bible impressed or disgusted, God's Word still accomplishes its intended purpose.[1] Of course, God's deepest desire is that people hear his plan, understand his Word, and are all-in from the depths of their souls.[2] So whether you trust God and his Word or are skeptical of his existence and his goodness, you can still glean much from this book. For a person doesn't need to know the difference between "Thoreau" and "thorough" to read a poem and still be moved by its lyric.

What is strikingly sad is that broken relationships are not solely limited to people who are ignorant of God's plan for them. To be honest, there are plenty of people who have no clue or care about the things of God, and they are making an absolute mess of the relationships in their lives. However, there are also those who have knowledge of the things of God—maybe they go to church, read their Bibles at home, and hear and understand what God says—and yet they also are making a mess of the relationships in their lives as well. There are even those who ought to be experts in the spiritual and relational field—such as church ministry leaders and even some pastors—who know intimately the things of God, and even they are resistant or inept at social reconciliation as well.

This last thought might lead us all to scratch our heads, throw in the towel of faith and friendship-improvement, and say, "Good grief! If not even pastors and 'good Christians' are loving and living in right relationships with others, then why even bother trying?!" A few perspectives on this thought are that first, there are no such things as "good Christians." Only forgiven ones. And second, brokenness and destruction are not different traps from those who "know-better" or who "ought-to-know-better" than those who don't.

I know of someone who had a bit of a backward application of grace toward others. They were more forgiving and excusing of the terrible things that people did if they didn't follow Jesus Christ—if they didn't believe in the purposes of God. "They don't know any different," was this person's reply. "They didn't know God's heart and God's desire. They weren't spiritually discerning enough to obey him."

---

1. See Isa 55:10–11; God's Word can lead a person to greater understanding and obedience to what is right—thus accomplishing its intent to the discerning and faithful heart. It can also be proven true through the scoffing and disobedient rejection of a mocker, leading a person to misery and a life of separation from gladness—likewise accomplishing its intent to the foolish and rejecting heart.

2. More on this in chapter 6, "A Healthy Foundation."

However, this person thought differently about a Christian—a follower of Jesus who claimed to seek his Word and follow his Way. If a *Christian* were caught in something that was disgusting and displeasing to God, then this person's opinion of them quickly changed to a different tune. "They ought to know better," they said. "They are being led by the Holy Spirit and they know God's Word. There is no excuse for those terrible things that they have done!"

The fundamental flaw with this kind of conditional justification is that it supposes that errors and disgraces are something that only certain people fall prey to. We clearly know plenty of individuals in our lives who play the counterexample to the impression that "good people ought to act well toward others." It often is those who are nearest to us that gouge us with the deepest wounds. This is not difficult to understand, because we *all*, as people, are plagued with the nature of sin and on our own are separate from God's way. Apart from Jesus, we are all just as lost. In fact, it is often those who are closest to Jesus who are *more* tempted and lured away, because Christ-followers are a direct threat to Christ's opposition.[3] The temptation to transgress God's perfect position is not any less for those who know it; rather, it is indeed more. As a result—not as a justification, but rather simply as an explanation—even pastors and other seemingly "strong Christians" can wreck relationships. (Don't forget: pastors are people, too.)

With regards to one of the last people mentioned, I happen to strikingly resemble that remark. As a pastor of a church—and the author of this book on the subject—I am definitely not saying that I'm perfect in all of my interactions with others. But I have seen the carnage of disobeying the words that Jesus speaks from the Bible about relationships. In my living, and relating, and preaching—and here in my writing—I am trying to specifically follow Jesus' words in my own life. Not only this, I am also trying to teach others to follow them as well.

I am certainly not an expert in my field in the sense that I presume to be (using the common cell phone texting abbreviation) "bff's" with the world. I am clearly not a person of perfection, as those who have had conflicts with me can rightly attest. There are undoubtedly people whom I have hurt and offended, and there are definitely people in my life who have hurt and offended me. After all, I am a grandson, son, uncle, cousin, nephew, brother, husband, father, friend, neighbor, co-worker, and pastor, living in a falling-apart world. I have had my fair share of relationship rifts in my lifetime. (The joke in my immediate family is this: as I am a former public high

3. In fact, the temptation of unforgiveness and the plan to destroy relationships is called one of " . . . [Satan's] designs"; see 2 Cor 2:11.

school teacher and a current preacher, and as my wife is an academically-trained public speaker, *no one* wins a fight in our house!)

A man in a pristine white suit shouting caution next to a muddy pit is less to be trusted than a man covered head-to-toe in that mud, climbing out of the pit, pleading with all other passers-by not to fall in.

∫

The ethos that I *do* have in writing this book, and the benefit that I offer to you—the reader—is that in all of my relationships, both close and distant, both good and bad, I have sought by God's grace in obedience to his Word to keep my relationships full of love and occasion for reconciliation. Though I cannot control whether this is reciprocated by others around me or not, I have at least embraced forgiveness and peace with everyone myself, seeking God's right ways of how we ought to live life together. And in all the relationship mess-ups I've made—and oh boy, have I made quite a few—I have learned, through God's grace, that I need to orient my heart compassionately with the desire to help people be kept from making those same mistakes in their relationships with others (and in their relationship with God as well). After all, a man in a pristine white suit shouting caution next to a muddy pit is less to be trusted than a man covered head-to-toe in that mud, climbing out of the pit, pleading with all other passers-by not to fall in.

Chapter 2

∫

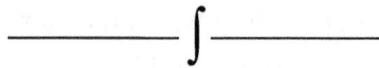

The Relations*l*ips Quiz

I AM A MAN. Normally that's not the most shockingly obvious statement in the world, but it is pertinent in context, given the fact that my firstborn son and I together are the *only men* in our immediate household. We are surrounded by a burgeoning blessing of beautiful women—my wonderful wife, and our three delightful daughters. The humor—and the honest truth in some respects—around our family is that in order to get away to keep our sanity, my son and I will be going to a *lot* of baseball games together. And I certainly don't mean any disrespect for the female readers of this book when I say this: reconciling hostile relationships in my family will take on a whole new meaning when menstrual synchrony is in full force in my home!

With all of the young ladies in our family, my son and I have been subject to our fair share of movies and video media with feminine themes. One of those favorite films in my family is Disney's *Frozen*. The movie is complete with its proverbially strong princesses, daring and handsome heroes, and cute and cuddly creatures. Interestingly enough, the movie has a relationship rift as one of the greatest dramatic conflicts throughout almost the entire movie. Not only do the two main characters—sisters, at that—struggle through relationship differences and irreconciliation in the plot, but one of the sub-plots is the insertion of a curious character named Kristoff and his unlikely best friend, a reindeer named Sven.

In the movie, Kristoff is a burly ice salesman who has been hurt and disenchanted with personal friendships and relationships in his past. As a result of this, he has willingly taken on a life of seclusion, with his only companion being his pal reindeer. In the movie, and in true cinematographic musical form, he even sings an impromptu duet with his (real in setting, but imaginary in talking) animal friend about how reindeers are better than people. It is a stroke of comical lyricism hearing the macho minstrel Kristoff strum and hum about his own broken relationships of the past, while mimicking the speech of his best friend, a hoofed animal.

As we catch a glimpse of Kristoff's relationship worldview, we can similarly relate to the fact that there are many things that people have done—or attitudes and actions that people have represented—which can lead many of us to purposefully distance ourselves from real, genuine, and authentic relationships with others. However, when we understand God's desires for our lives, we see that his intent for us on this earth is that we should not seek distance, but rather that we must run to eliminate the gaps in our interactions together. Otherwise, we would all think that singing real songs to imaginary talking creatures is the most fulfilling interaction that this world has to offer!

As we seek to live life together in a more God-honoring and divinely-inspiring way, we must also be confronted with many misnomers and errant presuppositions regarding relationships—specifically with regards to what the Bible says about human interaction and life together. In order to confront some of these errors and engage God's Word on the topic, I'd like to take you through a series of questions called "The Relationslips Quiz." How would you answer each of the following?

The Relationslips Quiz

QUESTION 1: True or False? The kind of love and compassion God has for us is different than the kind of feelings that we are to have for our enemies.

QUESTION 2: True or False? God is kind to the ungrateful and evil.

QUESTION 3: True or False? We are commanded to be like God in showing mercy to others.

QUESTION 4: True or False? Forgiving others is not necessary in order to be forgiven by God.

QUESTION 5: True or False? The phrase "Time heals all wounds" is a quote from Jesus in the Bible.

QUESTION 6: True or False? If we experience hurt from a Christian friend, we are justified to cease friendship and continue worshiping God in good conscience.

QUESTION 7: True or False? God desires that we get along with everyone in the church.

As a former public-school teacher, a current dad and mentor, and a forever student of God's Word, my nature is inclined to have some kind of grading scale or rubric for the Relationslips Quiz. If I were to create one, it might be something along the lines of:

> All 7 Correct = You are the world's best friend. Everybody loves you.

> 6–5 Correct = You are getting there. Keep trying harder, and people will love you more.

> 4–3 Correct = You are on the borderline of being dumped as a pal. Possibly consider additional study on being nice.

> 2–0 Correct = You are a merciless meanie. Nobody likes you. Go find a reindeer.

The reality is that the Relationslips Quiz is not meant to have an accompanying grading scale—the one above is simply for anecdotal humor's sake. In all seriousness, if there is *any way* in which we are misguided, incorrectly led, or errantly living, we must change and be renewed to embrace and pursue what is right. Not only do our misinterpretations and "presumptuous sins"[1] keep us from right relationships with others, but they also keep us from a right relationship with God. His desire is that we learn from him and be like him through believing in and following after Jesus Christ.

Further, the questions in this Relationslips Quiz are, of course, by no means exhaustive. Rather, they serve as a construct for us to look more closely at what Jesus has to say about our relationships together, and God's loving relationship with us. So, let us parse the questions and discuss the correct answers of the Relationslips Quiz, as guided and governed by God's Word, the Bible.

---

1. Ps 19:13. Additionally, if we don't shed willful sins and errant assumptions in our lives that are not governed by God's good Word, these errors will "have dominion over [us]," and subsequently also rule over our relationships with others as well.

Chapter 3

∫

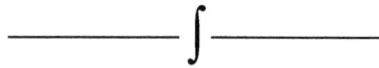

Moments of Truth

QUESTION 1: True or False?
The kind of love and compassion God has
for us is different than the kind of feelings
that we are to have for our enemies.

Answer: FALSE. Jesus says that we are to love our enemies with the exact kind of love that God has for us, which is an unconditional love. Let's look at this from Jesus' very own lips, in Luke 6:27, 35a[1]:

> "But I say to you who hear, Love your enemies, do good to those who hate you . . . But love your enemies, and do good, and lend, expecting nothing in return, and your reward will be great, and you will be sons of the Most High."

I love football. I love chocolate. I love my kids. I love the wintertime. In English, you all might think that I am crazy, or that I need to follow up my statements with further clarification (especially that last one, as the vast majority in the world would be just fine if summer annexed winter in a

---

1. What is meant by the "a" designation in a verse—such as "Luke 6:35a"—is in reference to the first part of the verse. Concurrently, "b" would refer to the second part of the verse (as in "Luke 6:35b," which will appear in the commentary with Relationships Quiz, Question 2).

hostile meteorological take-over). The limits of the English language do not give us very much in terms of synonyms for the word "love"—such as when "I love . . . " starts each of those very different statements that I made above. However in the Koine Greek language[2]—in which the New Testament of the Bible was originally written—there are a few different words for "love," and each of the Greek words represents a different kind (or at least a different context) of love—like the first quiz question hints at.

There is the kind of love that, in Greek, is represented by the word "eros." This is where we get the English word "erotic." It is the kind of romantic and sensual love that a husband and wife have, in a healthy marriage relationship. In the Greek language, it would be very inappropriate—and erroneous—to use "eros" to refer to love in the wrong setting, or toward the wrong person. For example, I love my wife, and I love my Grandmother. But I kiss my wife "Good Morning" on the lips very differently than I kiss my Grandma "Good Morning" on the cheek. (Technically speaking, my wife would prefer that I kept my "eros" morning-kisses away from her until after I have brushed my teeth from a long night of open-mouth snoring!) The kind of love I have for my wife is very different than the kind of love I have for my Grandma, even though in English I "love" them both.

There is another word for love, represented by the Greek word "phileo." You might be familiar with this from the prefix of that great historical American city named "Philadelphia," which literally means "The City of *Brotherly Love.*" "Phileo" is the kind of love that is brotherly—or sisterly—or a friendship-oriented love. Much different than "eros," the term "phileo" is a love that is very appropriate amongst friends. For all you male readers, especially those who are uncomfortable with broaching others' personal space and shy from greeting people with overtly-friendly touch, you can use the syllables in "phileo" (as in three syllables, "phi—le—o") to govern your bro-hugs . . . one-handed, shoulder-leaning, *three* smacks on the back. "Phi—le—o." Simply genius, if I do say so myself.[3]

---

2. "Koine Greek," meaning "common Greek," was the language/dialect spoken predominantly in the regions of Mesopotamia and Asia in which Jesus lived and where the New Testament of the Bible was written and flourished. This differs slightly from ancient/classical Greek—the likes of which Plato, Socrates, Aristotle, etc. spoke and wrote. Koine Greek is also a bit different from the Greek language that is written and spoken in Greece today.

3. Unfortunately, I don't have a mnemonic device to describe the friendly hugs that women give to one another . . . and honestly, as a man, I can't quite explain or understand it either. You ladies "phileo" *all over* each other when you get together! Quite impressive in the context of healthy friendships for the female gender . . . and quite intimidating for us macho guys that think there's nothing more manly than overweight men in tight pants and stretch-fitting jerseys clutching and falling on top of one another while trying to

And then there is another Greek word for love, which is "agape." This word for love represents *unconditional* love. I have heard it described like this: "agape" love is the "love that loves in spite of." In John 13:34–35, Jesus calls it the love in which we are to "love one another: *just as* I have loved you . . . " (emphasis mine). "Agape," this unconditional love, is the kind of love in which God loves you.

In the verses from Luke 6 that are mentioned in the paragraphs above, Jesus says from his own mouth that you are to "Love *your enemies*"—and he says it twice (once in verse 27 and once in verse 35). Generally, biblical repetition is a literary tactic of importance; meaning, "more-than-once" is code for "pay attention; he really means it." So, in Luke 6:27 and 35a, what kind of "love" does Jesus mean? Which Greek word for "love" does Jesus use for how we are to love our enemies? It is *"agape."* It is unconditional love. Jesus says that we are to love our enemies with the same kind of unconditional love that God has for us. If we are to love even our enemies in this way, imagine what life would be like if we loved our friends this way as well.[4]

QUESTION 2: True or False?
God is kind to the ungrateful and evil.

Answer: TRUE. Jesus says this verbatim, and uses it as an expectation for how we are to act toward everyone around us. We see this in Luke 6:35b:

> "But love your enemies . . . for he [God] is kind to the ungrateful and the evil."

Jesus has an expectation for us, so that we would be like God in how we love others, treat others, and act toward others. We will never attain to perfection in the ultimate qualities of God's supreme character, but God makes explicitly clear that this should not deter us from this godly pursuit. In the same way in John 13:34 that Jesus says *"Just as I"* have loved others, so we are to do the same; likewise, Luke 6:35 speaks to the same thing as well. God shows kindness to those who think nothing of him, and he does this partially as an example for us to follow.

---

chase an inflatable ball made of the same material as our wives' Coach handbags (dudes, in case you missed it, I'm talking about the sport of football). Anyone who doesn't think that God has a sense of humor needs to be more attentive when their eyes are open!

4. This is also seen, quite clearly, in John 13:34–35, which was mentioned earlier. Here, Jesus' love for his disciples is the same—"agape"—as the love that Jesus commands to each other. Furthermore, in John 13:34, the designation "Just as I" drives the point home: precisely like God loves us, we are to love others, too.

In the great classic Broadway musical, *Les Misérables*, from the book by the same title written by Victor Hugo, there is an interesting interaction between the main character and a secondary character of great conscience. In the musical, Jean Valjean appears at the door of Bishop Charles-Francois-Bienvenu Myriel, seeking respite during the nighttime hours. This kind priest takes a risk and gives lodging for the night to the stranger, Valjean, only to discover in the morning that Valjean has fled and fleeced him of all the precious silverware in the pantry. A few scenes later, Valjean is apprehended by the authorities and forced to return to the bishop in order to pay his amends. When there, the bishop replies strangely: telling the officers that he actually gave permission for Valjean to take the silver pieces; in addition, he volunteers to give Valjean the silver candlesticks that the crooked con "forgot" to take the first time.

Readers of this great script and viewers of the masterful musical might find it ironic and counterintuitive that a "religious man" would not only allow a common criminal to steal from him, but additionally that he would give even *more* plunder to the ungrateful thief. However, a truer reflection of Hugo's work interprets the Bishop Bienvenu—aptly translated "Bishop Welcome" in English—in this way: in giving Valjean mercy in the form of the silver, the priest had actually paid some kind of ransom in order to steer Valjean to future good.

It is very clear, from the Bible, that silver and gold cannot ransom anyone from evil and into a right relationship in the presence of God. Only the all-sufficient sacrifice of Jesus Christ on the cross will satisfy the severity of our sin and provide salvation for all who believe in him. In terms of human interaction, however, the bishop in *Les Misérables* illustrated a remarkable precept: as God has shown common grace[5] to all people, we have the same opportunity to show kindness and grace to others as well. It may have been lofty in Hugo's story to think that a priest's lie, a scapegoat, and silver candlesticks might have changed a man's life forever. However, how much more incredible is it to think that our own kind actions and attitudes toward others might be used by God as pointers leading people to the kindness and grace that God shows to us through Jesus Christ.

---

5. "Common grace" is a term used to reference the kindness of God upon all people. The sunrise on every new day, breath in our lungs, the abilities within our bodies, etc.—these are all examples of God's "common grace." This differs, of course, from God's "saving grace," available to all but shown only to those who believe by faith in Jesus Christ for salvation; see Eph 2:1–10.

QUESTION 3: True or False?
We are commanded to be like God in showing mercy to others.

Answer: TRUE. In the same way that God shows mercy to us, we are like-wise to be merciful to other people, regardless of whether they are kind or merciful in return. We can see this in Luke 6:36, where Jesus says:

> "Be merciful, even as your Father [God] is merciful."

Some people have a soft impression of Jesus. With attributes that he demonstrates like love, compassion, and mercy—which the world today perceives to be generally effeminate or emasculating—many people think of Jesus as a kind of sissy Savior. The way that I see Jesus—and the way that he is portrayed historically—is as the incarnate God-man whose body was powerful and strong enough to endure an early career in ancient Near Eastern architecture[6], long-distance low-budget and low-diet travel, and a culmination of beatings and grueling wrongful execution death by cruci-fixion. He was no wimp. Nor were his words. In Luke 6:36, Jesus lays the law down. Even in his call for us to show mercy, Jesus packs the punch by calling everyone to hold to the relational expectations and standards of the almighty and omnipotent God.

Wimps beware. Although you might think that "be[ing] merciful" is something easy, society and our experience shows us that it can sometimes be more challenging than a triathlon. And showing mercy has no gender or demographic bias, either. Mini-van moms ready for fisticuffs at their tod-dler's junior squirt soccer games need to heed the high call of Jesus in show-ing mercy just like Boston Red Sox fans who break out with an anti-Yankees chant in the middle of early-season baseball games against the Kansas City Royals (yes, the angst is thick even in the presence of an irrelevant team that is not even from the state of New York). These examples, even in their harsh-ness or humor, are relatively tame compared to others that you might be able to think of on your own. So, before anyone trends toward thinking that Jesus is soft and that his words are weak, I encourage you to think again.

---

6. Jesus was known as "the carpenter's son" (Matt 13:55) as well as "the carpenter" (Mark 6:3), an easy presumption given that Joseph, Jesus' earthly fatherly caregiver, likely passed along his own trade to the rest of the male family members. Since the Greek work for "carpenter" can also be used to refer to any craftsman or manual la-borer, and since the primary architectural medium of that part of the world was brick or stone or other heavy materials, it could be just as likely that Jesus was a kind of stoneworker or heavy-brick builder; probably not at all different from a modern day concrete pourer or general construction worker. Jesus was no soft cookie nonetheless.

With a more proper understanding that Jesus gives us a higher "call of duty" than the video game of the same name, I hope that some of you will be up for the tough task of showing mercy. All of us need to be. For others, your hurts have pulverized you too deeply—or seemingly so—that you believe you cannot hold to the benchmark of divine mercy that Jesus demands for us. However, when we understand that *Jesus desires that we become more like him and less like those who hurt us*, it can lead us to muster strength and humbleness in embracing life how God lives it.

If we think about it, one tiny word found in what Jesus says in the verse above is radically amazing: the potent and perspective-changing word "as" (or possibly the two words "even as"). Jesus says that we are to be merciful "even as" whom? Jesus' call and command are that he wants for us to be like whom exactly? He wants us to be like God. In showing mercy to others, Jesus wants for us to be God-like. That is not sissy; that is pretty boss. Jesus' desire and challenge is for us to be like God with those around us.

We must all be well aware of the fact that we can never be exactly like God in every facet of our lives—nor should we have the pride as such, either. As Ecclesiastes 5:2 says so poignantly, " . . . for God is in heaven and you are on earth."[7] However in our perspectives on life, as we are here on earth living life with others, and as we might encounter difficulties in our relationships with others, let us not forget the One who watches over us from above. In other words, when you are looking *out* at your relationships with others, *don't forget to look up!* Having God's perspective is both humbling and empowering at the same time.

If we keep this in mind—that we are to make every effort to be like God in showing love, mercy, and compassion in our relationships with others—then this has the legitimately divine potential to heal our own hearts when we are hurt, and it just might improve our own relationships with others through hardships and happiness alike. Not only this, but a healthy perspective on mercy will also help us understand the rest of the questions on this Relations*l*ips Quiz. So, let's continue.

QUESTION 4: True or False?
Forgiving others is not necessary in order to be forgiven by God.

This answer might surprise you: the answer is FALSE. In other words, forgiving others *is* necessary. We *must* forgive others if we desire *any* forgiveness from God.

---

7. Meaning, "there is *much* distance and difference between humankind and God" (also, there ought to be *much* reverence and honor given to the God who is over all things).

Now, a bit of clarification may be needed so that nobody misunderstands what I am saying, and what the Bible is saying. It could cause us some philosophical and theological gymnastics to discern which comes before what: our forgiveness of others, and God's forgiveness for us. And my statement above may make it seem as if us forgiving others is a precursory and prerequisite step to us experiencing God's forgiveness for us. However, you may be misinterpreting my statement above, and the truth of God's Word that we will see below. For truly, in order to write a legible sentence in the English language (or any other language for that matter), one thing must be stated before the other! However, the reality is that both types of forgiveness are at work together, collectively, within the life of the Christian. Allow for me to explain further.

It is not as if God is in heaven as a learner, and we are on earth as the instructors; as if God is observing us forgiving others, and then saying to himself, "Ahhh, so *that's* how it works! I see! Looks like I'll follow suit and forgive them as well, then." That is not the case, and it never will be. It is also not as if God is in heaven as a merit-giving observer; as if God is watching us forgive others—or not forgive others—and then himself doling out forgiveness to us when we give it on earth one-for-one, and withholding forgiveness when we are stingy the same. No, no, it ain't so. In either of those false presumptions, God would be ignorant and impotent, and ungracious to boot—and the Bible is clear that our salvation is not obtained through merit, but rather it is extended simply by God's grace. However, what is true about God and us, and what is seen from a biblical worldview—not only what is observable from the Bible but also what is evident in the congruency of the truest Christian life—is that *if* we genuinely have experienced God's love and forgiveness personally ourselves, *then* a necessary outcome and byproduct of that forgiveness will be the extension of forgiveness to others. As it has been aptly said: "the forgiven person is the forgiving person."[8]

Forgiveness is a necessary fruit of a Christian. If you are unwilling to forgive others, then you may not truly have a fruit-filled relationship with Jesus Christ. We see this in Luke 6:37:

> "Judge not, and you will not be judged; condemn not, and you will not be condemned; forgive, and you will be forgiven."

We can also see this in Matt 6:14–15, which says:

> "For if you forgive others their trespasses, your heavenly Father will also forgive you, but if you do not forgive others their trespasses, neither will your Father forgive your trespasses."

8. Begg, *Forgiving and Forgiven, Part One.*

This is also articulated in Eph 4:32:

> "Be kind to one another, tenderhearted, forgiving one another,
> as God in Christ forgave you."

In the Ephesians passage above, it is clear that *because* God has forgiven us in Jesus Christ (for those of us who trust in Christ alone for life and God's forgiveness), then we are commanded—indeed, *it is necessary*—to forgive others. In Luke and Matthew, in both parallels of the same sermon message of Jesus, it is stated as being a matter of measure. In other words, how we forgive others will be a measure of how we will be forgiven. Or, stated another way: how we forgive others will be an *indicator* of the measure of God's forgiveness that we have truly believed and received.

In Matthew, Jesus' words about the necessity of forgiveness come right after what we know as "The Lord's Prayer," in which Jesus shows as central our need to be forgiven by God in heaven "as we also have forgiven our debtors" here on earth (Matt 6:12). They are put together in wonderful poetry:

> "'Forgive our sins as we forgive,'
> You taught us, Lord, to pray,
> But You alone can grant us grace
> To live the words we say.
>
> How can Your pardon, reach, and bless
> The unforgiving heart
> That broods on wrongs and will not let
> Old bitterness depart?
>
> In blazing light Your cross reveals
> The truth we dimly knew:
> What trivial debts are owed to us,
> How great our debt to You!
>
> Lord, cleanse the depths within our souls
> And bid resentment cease.
> Then, bound to all in bonds of love,
> Our lives will spread Your peace."[9]

C.S. Lewis, the Christian author, storyteller, and theologian, has this wonderful quote from his book *The Weight of Glory*. In it he describes the Christian life relative to the topic of forgiveness by saying, "To be a Christian means to forgive the inexcusable, because God has forgiven the

---

9. Herklots, "Forgive Our Sins as We Forgive," 94.

inexcusable in you."[10] Allow me to put this into modern-day language: if you call yourself a "Christian," but you are not forgiving others when they have done wrong against you, then I'm afraid you're going to have to change your religious affiliation. Because "Christian" is just not the word to describe you.

Now, I don't at all mean to take away from Jesus Christ's powerful saving work on the cross. I don't believe that C.S. Lewis means to minimize this wonderful atoning sacrifice either. I am not intending to place additional requirements added on to God's completely sufficient unconditional love and his grace given through Jesus. Rather, in seeking to grapple with Jesus' own words which show that we will not be forgiven unless we forgive—and in understanding that heaven will have no entrants with unforgiven sins as baggage—we see that a more complete picture of a Christian is someone who experiences the magnitude of God's forgiveness upon them, and then is glad to extend forgiveness to all others as a result.

> "To be a Christian means to forgive the inexcusable, because God has forgiven the inexcusable in you." (C.S. Lewis)

∫

If we understand forgiveness in comparison, we begin to arrive more deeply at what I believe C.S. Lewis is saying. We should not try to trivialize forgiveness, or grade it based upon the severity of sins committed; rather, we must see forgiveness as a character demonstration of our souls. It is true that our sins against God, without Jesus' payment for them and God's forgiveness of them, will keep us out of heaven. On the other hand, other peoples' sins against us, without our forgiveness for them and the reconciliation of a fractured friendship, will simply keep these people out of our living room. Though there certainly may be many more severe wrongs done to you than my trite anecdotes do justice, the principle of forgiveness is still not negated based on the severity of wrongs.[11] For in reality, the gravity of the compilation of our sins against God make any other collection of sins by others against us pale in comparison. We ought to find it much easier to

10. Lewis, *The Weight of Glory*, 181–83.

11. More on the topic of forgiveness, namely the severity of wrongs done to us and the perspective of God, is dealt with in chapter 5, "Relations*lip* Objections," later in this book.

forgive others for their miniscule offenses, compared to the immensity of our depravity for which we have been forgiven by God.

Jesus gives another anecdotal illustration of forgiveness in Matt 18:21–35 to prove the point well. A man had fallen deeply in debt to a very wealthy and prominent king. When the king called everyone to account, the man undoubtedly could not pay his share—valued at tens of millions of dollars, if not more. Even though the custom of the time was for the indebted person and their family to be either imprisoned or sold into slavery until the debt was recouped—which in this man's case would have been probably for the rest of his life—the king instead showed pity and forgiveness toward the sorrowful groveling debtor, and eliminated his debt.

Just a short time later, the forgiven man—free and full of joy, having received a new lease on life—found a pal who owed him only a couple hundred bucks. He pressed his friend for the money, which the friend did not have, and as consequence he had him thrown in jail until his measly debt could be repaid. The whole situation reeked of hypocrisy and ingratitude, and word of it all eventually came back to the king.

The king, now less forgiving and rightly indignant, made a teachable moment out of this unforgiving man. He was just recently forgiven an inordinate amount of money, but was unwilling to forgive a much more meager sum. As consequence, the king re-instituted the massive debt and subjugated the man to prison until it was paid. The moral of the story: "So also my heavenly Father will do to every one of you, if you do not forgive your brother from your heart" (Matt 18:35).

Would a loving God do such a harsh thing to such lowly people as us, if we happen to find it difficult to forgive someone for wronging us? Well, the beautiful benefit of Jesus' parables is that they illustrate for its readers a situation *in advance*, so that the parables can help their readers avoid those situations in their own lives. It is just like us owning insurance on a car or home or personal property: it is something we have in front of us, but it is something we hope to never have to use. Jesus tells a tale about the perils of unforgiveness so that you and I can *avoid it*. Especially in light of the incredible forgiveness shown to us by God, we are comparably able to choose to extend forgiveness to others—and thereby never need to face knowing or experiencing God's consequence ourselves for not forgiving.

In all things, let us not forget again that regarding relationships with others around you, it would do us well to *look up*. Has God forgiven you so that you can choose to not forgive others? Never is it so. If God is willing to forgive you, then he also wants you to be willing to forgive others, no matter what they have done and no matter how hard of a task forgiving others might be.

QUESTION 5: True or False?
The phrase "Time heals all wounds" is a quote from Jesus in the Bible.

Answer: FALSE. This is neither a quote from Jesus, nor is it found anywhere in the Bible. Hence, "time heals all wounds" is non-biblical. In fact, it would not be a stretch to say that this idea is in fact *un*-biblical.[12]

People by and large tend to walk the path of least resistance. We do what is easiest and most preferable for us, and not what is difficult (even if what is the harder thing to do is the right thing). That is why most people lie when caught doing something wrong. That is why women farm out the trash-collection chores to their husbands. That is why my wife asks for me to cook bacon. (Little known fact: cooking bacon is one of my wife's least favorite things on the planet. To be fair to her, if this simple task tops her "Lifetime Discomfort List," then I'm quite the blessed man in our marriage and our house.)[13] This is also why people are not quick to trudge through messy conflict in pursuit of reconciliation, and why they avoid spending time with those who are difficult to get along with. We are more apt to be governed by "time heals all wounds," since it is easier, and we hope that this perspective is honorable and possibly even biblical. The fact is that it is neither.

We as human beings gravitate toward this natural "time heals all wounds" model of relationships and conflict resolution much more than healthy, respectful, and biblical forms of reconciliation. Though I might not be an expert on why people have rotten relationships, I suspect that people like to let time pass and hope that the brain forgets because it is seemingly a simpler task than walking the hard road of confessing our wrongs and forgiving others for what they have done to us. A companion phrase to "time heals all wounds," therefore, might be the similarly-maligned perspective: "ignorance is bliss."

The fact of the matter is that although our minds might not be able to recall hurts in the past as clearly as the present, our hearts have a much more indelible memory. Just because we think that a delay in time could cause people to come back together again, this doesn't mean that an intentionally

---

12. The designation "non-biblical" means "not found in the Bible." There are many things today that are "non-biblical"—such as automobiles and cheeseburgers. However, it doesn't necessarily designate cars and bacon cheddar sliders as contrary to the will of God (unless, of course, God the Holy Spirit speaks through your doctor's visit, calling you to diet and exercise). What *is* against God's plan for our lives and relationships are things that are "*un*-biblical," which means "*against* God's desires as seen in his Word, the Bible."

13. I am reminded of the words of a friend of mine who, on my wedding day told me, "Jason, just remember: you married *up*!" He could not have been more correct.

passive restoration is healthy or that a lethargic process of reconciliation is honoring to God. If anything, letting time pass before forgiving others and making relationships better allows for laziness and the scapegoat of being slack and not loving unconditionally, confessing honestly, or forgiving completely. Additionally, it actually gives the devil an opportunity to breed more hurt and distance in our friendships.

There was a counselor who was helping a couple through some difficult relationships within their family. In the process of the counseling session, the distraught couple frequently referenced hurts in the past as key obstacles in getting the family members together. "And then three years ago, they did this . . . and then at the last family reunion, they said that . . . and last Christmas, they didn't even call . . . " This was an instance of not only the heart's memory being as clear as a bell, but also their mind's recollection being crystal as well. In their unwillingness to forgive what was done in the past, *this couple* was actually primarily responsible for the distance in their family—not all the other family members that they thought or blamed. Because the couple let time pass as opposed to pursuing healing sooner, and because time did not heal their wounds—since it does *not* do so—they allowed hurt to be continually re-processed in their relationships more than the original hurts that were done to them in the past.

A wonderful precept that tracks much closer with biblical reconciliation is "don't go to bed angry." This is recommended by psychologists and pastors alike in premarital counseling to young couples, and it is a common colloquialism of what the Bible says in Eph 4:26b–27:

> "Do not let the sun go down on your anger, and give no opportunity to the devil."

The Jewish and ancient Near East calendar is much different from that in the Western Hemisphere. One of the primary ways that our time-telling differs is in terms of the beginning and the end of a day. For most of us reading this book with a western-chronological perspective (and since this book's first printing is in the English language, it is likely that if you are reading this with a command of English, that is you!), we recognize that a day begins at sun*rise*, and henceforth the next day likewise begins once the nighttime from sunset-on has ended and the sun has peeked over the horizon in the sky at the next morning. In some ancient cultures—which includes the Bible's original authorship and readership—a day actually began at sun*set*.[14] So one day

---

14. One of the earliest accounts of this can be seen at the Bible's earliest mention of the notion of a "day"—in Gen 1. There, as God outlines each created day's contents, it concludes "And there was *evening* and there was *morning*, the first [and second, third, etc.] day" (emphasis mine). In the ancient Near East and current

to the next would have been considered "from evening to evening" (or more precisely "from evening to morning," but you get the idea). Therefore, we see a cultural nuance being drawn out here from Eph 4 about "not let[ting] the sun go down on your anger." I believe what is being said is so much more than simply "don't go to bed angry"—although that is certainly a serviceable modern application of this verse of the Bible (which is a stark contrast of many people's beliefs that "I'll just sleep it off and go to bed angry. Maybe it'll all go away in the long run." Sounds a lot like the common and false notion of "time heals all wounds" to me!). What I think God instructs us is better: "Do not let the sun go down . . . in other words, don't even let *another day go by* with you being unreconciled with another."

If there are people reading this book who like to remain angry, or who find it difficult to let go of their hurt emotions, or who are trying to justify their unreconciled behavior, they might press pause at this point in the book and play a sneaky game of Thesaurus-Limbo with God's Word. "Well, I understand that we shouldn't go to bed angry . . . but I'm not *angry*. I'm just *upset*. Or *hurt*. Or *wounded* by what someone else did to me." That's like a friend who, in humor, said "I'm not mean; I'm just insensitive." The wording used might be different, but the truth is still the same.

The verbiage doesn't need to be spot-on in terms of the description or explanation of your emotions. It could be anger, hurt, resentment, frustration, irritation, or any other synonym. Rather than trying to rebut the Bible in our defense, why don't we all put down the thesaurus and understand what is being said: if you allow even a *single new day* to pass without being reconciled, then you are effectively giving the devil a foothold to wreak havoc in your life. Sadly so, because many people have bought in to the philosophy that "time heals all wounds," we are allowing the devil to not only have a foothold but take over the entire ladder to our hearts. Rather than this, why don't we forgive like we have been forgiven, love like we have been loved, and let go of our hurts before they plague us yet one more day? It might be easier said than done, to be honest; however, it is still something of great consequence to be done all the same.

Middle Eastern culture, a day was not considered "morning-noon-and-night," but rather "evening-morning-and-noon."

QUESTION 6: True or False?
If we experience hurt from a Christian friend,
we are justified to cease friendship and continue
worshiping God in good conscience.

Answer: FALSE. Jesus says that instead of carrying around hurt from others—or knowing that we have hurt others—we are to drop what we are doing *first* and pursue a reconciled relationship with the one whom there have been wrongs.

This Relations*l*ips Quiz question can have some connection to the previous one about "time healing all wounds" and holding on to unforgiveness inside of us—or moving on without trying to make it right. In the context of Christian friendships in the church—the body of Christ—we see Jesus raising the ante of letting time pass in Matt 5:23–24, when he says:

> "So if you are offering your gift at the altar and there remember that your brother has something against you, leave your gift there before the altar and go. First be reconciled to your brother, and then come and offer your gift."

In the ancient Hebrew community, a person bringing a sacrifice to the altar at the temple or in the sanctuary was often synonymous with worshiping God. With Matt 5 in view, we can apply the verses as if they are saying: "If you are going to church and realize that somebody has some beef with you, pause your Sunday morning activity and get together one-on-one with that person. Confess any wrongs and forgive each other in biblical unity, and then you may come on in and take part in the church's worship service."

Yet instead of obeying and applying Jesus' own words in church, there are many people who enter into a sanctuary or worship center week after week, bringing a bone to pick with someone there. Sure, it may not be evident and overt in the middle of the praise and worship music or the pastor's sermon. The point is that it's still there . . . and Jesus says regarding worship, there ought to be *none*. Instead of everyone putting on their "Sunday face"[15] and coming to church seemingly full of cheer, Jesus' encouragement might be more that we kindly seek out people in the church lobby who we think

---

15. The term and idea of someone's "Sunday face" is the all-too-frequent practice of hiding our honest emotions and situations from those who ought to be most equipped and available to meet our hearts' deepest needs (for more, see Larry Crabb's *Connecting* and *The Safest Place on Earth*.) Instead, people often put on "my face on Sunday," masquerading as if there was nothing wrong and if they had no care in the world. This "Sunday-face" practice is yet another thing causing relationships to slip into distance, disagreement, and distress.

might be frustrated or irked at us, and we graciously ask them, "Hey, can I talk to you privately before we go into worship?" Rather than our worship centers and sanctuaries being packed with hypocrites, Jesus would prefer that our church parking lots and lobbies be loaded with reconcilers. *Then* we could all enter in true gladness and grace, ready to worship God for the same grace that he gives to us.

Even though many think and believe that the number of church members in a congregation is an indicator of God's blessing, and although megachurch ministries are all the rage, I would say that based on my experiences in churches and parachurch ministries of many different sizes, biblical reconciliation in agreement with Matt 5 is likely not easier in megachurches than smaller congregations; it is likely more difficult. That is because in large congregations and jam-packed worship centers where people can easily disappear into the crowd, the "Sunday-face" masquerade is more convenient for people in that larger crowd, and the temptation to hide hurts and irreconciliation may be greater there as well. The un-biblical "time heals all wounds" is generally harder to pull off in smaller church congregations unless the masquerade make-up is laid on very thick, or there is deeper dysfunction in the church congregation as a whole.

Although it is an excellent practice for closer fellowship and relational connections in large churches to be facilitated through small groups, this often doesn't automatically lead to healing with those who worship with gripes on Sunday mornings (or Saturday nights, or whenever worship services are held). Small groups are spectacular but remember that we as people—as well as we Christians (Christians are still people, correct?)—are more apt to do what is easiest than us doing what is most right. Those who come to church angry—or upset, or insert-your-own-preferred-synonym-for-"anger"-here—are less apt to join a small group under their own volition (or they are less apt to become vulnerable and transparent even if they are part of one). Avoiding relations*l*ips and pursuing healthy biblical relationships takes effort and obedience to God's Word, and often some training to avoid the triage of relational baggage. Embracing the Bible on the subject, and being committed to pursuing healthy living together, both are prerequisites to similarly healthy worship and relational community.

Whether churches are small or large, the idea of transparency was much more applicable in early church history when the number of church congregations was fewer. In the early church after Jesus' death, resurrection, and ascension into heaven, there was generally only one Christian community—one local church—in each city or town where the gospel had spread. As there weren't other churches right around the corner, if two people had a falling-out in the same church family, the options were to either (a) reconcile their relationship before worshiping together again (which is, of course, Jesus' preferable recommendation and requisite command in Matt 5:23–24), or (b) see that one—or both—feuding persons leave the church in entirety. If there was a conflict between people in the church in the Grecian city of Corinth in the early history of the Christian church, for example, since there was only one church in that entire city, there was no other choice but to reconcile relationships—or face self-imposed exile from that city's only church community as a natural consequence. Leaving the church due to unreconciled relationships would have most certainly left the relational vagabond to spiral into deeper spiritual decay and interpersonal loneliness as time passed, which would have been a strong motivating factor for the two hurting parties to restore their relationship and return to active worship in the church.

As the good news of Jesus Christ has spread across the globe, and as churches in some parts of the world are now as frequent as street corners, I wonder if the hard work of obedience in biblical reconciliation has paid the price.[16] Today, besides the church-feud options (a) and (b) that I mentioned from the ancient Near Eastern culture above, there is now another all too familiar option available: (c) to leave one church with conflict in our hearts, and join another church down the road as a silent welcomed hero. "Time heals all wounds," with the frequency of churches on every corner, fueled by our temptation to not engage in the hard road of biblical reconciliation as seen in Matt 5 and elsewhere, has led to many churches welcoming in biblically disobedient Sunday morning worshipers into their membership. If we as individuals shed this notion that with time comes healing, and instead recognize that with *immediacy* and with *forgiveness* comes healing (which is what we see in Eph 4 and Matt 5), then our churches—both mega- and mini—would become more healthy and transparent in the manner that Christ calls them to be. And so would our relationships be as well.

A word on how Matt 5:23–24 can speak practically to *how* we make wronged relationships right: the word "reconciled" that Jesus used means "to renew a friendship with someone." It also carries with it a subtle nuance of *changing* or *transforming* yourself in order to make the relationship

---

16. I gladly celebrate the spread of the gospel and the expanse of churches and church planting—new churches beginning—across the globe. What I mean by "biblical reconciliation paying the price" is that what seems to be more likely is our comfort and our address of worship taking sway over our conviction for obeying the Bible. People are more comfortable leaving churches angry and attending another church across town, rather than staying in one church and reconciling at all costs because that is Christ's command in Scripture. The gospel-spread and prevalence of new churches is fooling us into becoming disobedient and biblically lazy. Instead, we should adhere to obedience and celebrate the gospel all the same.

right. In other words, if there is a conflict between you and someone else, and you take the initiative to get together and sit down and talk with that person with whom who you need to be reconciled, it will yield absolutely *zero benefit or relational fruit* for you and them if you just *stayed the same* and simply rehashed your former beef. In order for there to be progress and growth and a relationship tilt, then it will require a bit of change from one person—or likely both. In addition, this change and get-together-ness might not lead to all of the world's problems being solved in just one sitting. In fact, it might not even mean that all of your problems between *each other* are solved or resolved over one meeting or one cup of coffee! However, if what is desired is that each person commits to *make a change*[17] in how they are feeling or thinking toward one another, then the relationship can begin to be reconciled as Jesus desires. Forgiving, loving unconditionally, and re-newing a friendship are all necessary prerequisites *before* you spend time with others in the presence of God.

Just one more thing about corporate worship and time spent in church: as a current pastor, former worship leader, and prior church ministry vol-unteer, I can offer some interesting insight into the goings-on of a regular Sunday morning routine in many churches. There are many volunteers who rise early on Sundays to help prepare a church service: from people getting significant things ready such as setting up the entire sound system and stage for worship, to those doing simple things like making the coffee and arrang-ing delicious pastries that are eaten in the church lobby or fellowship hall. There are church administrative staff who ensure that the church bulletin and newsletter are free from type-o's and are helpful to everyone entering the church that week. There are custodians and janitorial workers who cut the grass (or clear the snow, depending on which season and region of the country in which you live), and who do such unsightly things like wash the toilets and take out the trash so that the church building is presentable each week. There are worship team musicians who rehearse and recite a week's worth of lyrics and music in practice and preparation for leading the congregation through worship in song. There are children's ministry work-ers and helpers who review lessons and prepare crafts to teach and disciple kids and youth. There are morning Bible study and Sunday school teach-ers who facilitate prayer requests and pore over biblical teachings for their class attendees. And contrary to the notion that pastors only work one day a week, there are faithful ministers and preachers who diligently study and write their sermons and illustrations all week for long hours, praying that they will be as impactful as they have worked hard for them to be. There are

17. More on this can be found in chapter 4, "Get Ready for Some Changes."

many people who prepare much and who often do so all week in order to get ready for a weekend worship service.

And then there is the average church attendee . . . who doesn't prepare *one bit* before walking in to church.

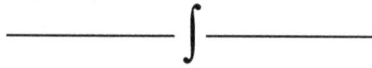

Who is to say that countless volunteers and church staff are supposed to work hard, prepare harder, and plan even harder still for an energetic and enthusiastic Sunday morning worship service, but everyone else in the church family or community doesn't have to prepare a lick before walking past the greeters in the lobby and sitting down in their seat in church? In his book, *How To Walk Into Church,*[18] author Tony Payne shares poignantly that even though there aren't common normal necessary prerequisites for the average person coming to church, maybe there ought to be. It is somewhat hypocritical to think that the pastor, or the worship team, or the children's ministry workers, or the hospitality helpers ought to be doing a lot of work in preparation for church worship services (sometimes all week long, as we pastors *work very hard almost every day of the week,* including Sundays!), yet those who come to receive the fruits of their labor have no obligation in return.

There are many people who prepare much in order to get ready for a weekend worship service. . .and then there is the average church attendee, who doesn't prepare one bit before walking in to church.

∫

I wonder how church attendees would respond if their pastor got up on stage some Sunday and said, "Welp, Friends, *just like you,* I didn't really do anything to get myself ready for church today. Let's see, what should I talk about for my sermon . . . !" And I know that there are those who will immediately jump to the argument that says, "Well, pastor, you get *paid* to prepare sermons. You get *paid* to lead ministries. You get *paid* to make sure church runs without a hitch. You get *paid* to do stuff like that! It's your *job!*" However, children's ministry helpers, and Bible study teachers, and worship team members, and even coffee-and-pastry-preppers *do not* get

18. Payne, *How to Walk Into Church.*

paid to do their hard work getting ready for church on Sunday (and quite honestly, thousands of bi-vocational pastors and itinerant ministers actually do *not* get paid to lead in ministry, either). In fact, the times in church ministry where I have wondered if congregational mutiny might ensue was not founded on whether my sermon was spot-on or sour for that week, but rather was based on whether there was enough freshly-brewed jo' and yummy munchies in the entryway beforehand! In all seriousness, I wonder how God feels when he sees people pouring into church each weekend, *not getting ready or being prepared* for going there. Matt 5:23–24 gives us some simple benchmark preparations and prerequisites for corporate worship that everyone ought to follow. And as Payne writes, maybe there ought to be other requirements for walking into church as well.

QUESTION 7: True or False?
God desires that we get along with everyone in the church.

Answer: TRUE. By this time in the answer-reveal of this Relations*l*ips Quiz, it shouldn't surprise you that *maybe* the answer is contrary to what the proverbial bitter heart might expect. And given the answers to some of the quiz questions above, this one by now should be a no-brainer. After all, if we are called to even *love* everyone with the kind of unconditional love that God loves us, then certainly a somewhat lesser relational task—like getting along with others—is a "true" all the same. But not only are God's desires that we get along with others, He additionally expects that we are constantly working at it.

Now, I don't suggest that we need to all be clones of everyone else around us and hold to the same kind of doctrinal or ideological views similarly to others around us—even in church. I remember a friend who, after church one Sunday, was sharing about how much he appreciated the sermon that the pastor preached . . . even though he only agreed theologically with three out of the five main points in the message. All the same, this friend still loved the pastor, and got along with him very well. So, when using the phrase "get along," I don't specifically mean "have the same views along with" everyone. However, even in differences of opinion or belief, we must always have right relationships with everyone—especially those in the church.

You can see this specifically in Romans 12:18, which says:

> "If possible, so far as it depends on you, live peaceably with all."

This verse is such a relational lynchpin in so many ways, for it packs a reconciliatory punch in just over a dozen words. It is in many respects the closest thing biblically to the adage "you can lead a horse to water, but you cannot make it drink." Rom 12:18 says that you may not be able to control whether or not others are living peaceably with you, but "if possible, so far as it depends on you," you and I must live peaceably with others. But here specifically, I want for the "peaceable living" to be what is held in view. It is God's desire for us to have calm, reconciled, forgiving, confessing, unconditionally loving, unifying, and peaceable living with *everyone*. And last I checked the church was included.

Another great biblical reference for this is found in 2 Cor 13:11, which says:

> "Finally, brothers [and sisters, by application], rejoice. Aim for restoration, comfort one another, agree with one another, live in peace; and the God of love and peace will be with you."

How many of us would desire for God to be with us? How many of us would desire for God's love to be with us? How about God's peace to be with us? How about God's love and peace, *and* the God who *grants us* that love and peace, being with us? Then according to 2 Cor 13:11, we must first be peaceful and restoring and agreeable with one another. If this verse is a genuine cause-and-effect—which textually seems to be credibly so—then we must first demonstrate our peaceableness with others before God will grant his presence and love and peace to us. And, in light of our understanding of the other Relationslips Quiz questions and explanations above, it seems very right and complementary for God to hold to the same consistent standards as he always has:

> "Love others, forgive others, be peaceful with others . . . and I [God speaking] will be peaceful, forgiving, and loving toward you."

Chapter 4

∫

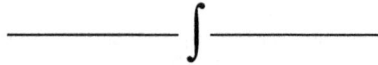

Get Ready for Some Changes

I DIDN'T KNOW IT when I began to write these important "life-together" principles, but what I have found is that in articulating this idea and writing this book, I have become quite alliterate. No, that's not "illiterate," meaning "unable to read," otherwise I would not be a sensical author (and you would not even be able to read these words!). Alliteration is that special gift that pastors and preachers and speakers are somehow innately given to be able to string all kinds of related words together that start with the same letter. Even though we are often told to "avoid alliteration always," it never fails. It creeps in there.

The Relations*lips* alliteration that I am referring to, however, is genuinely circumstantial and unintentional (with the exception of the made-up nomenclature of the title of this book as a whole . . . *that* was on purpose). There just happen to be a lot of "r-words" when it comes to living in a healthy manner with others. Relationships—not relations*lips*—are sustained when people are reconciled, and repent of their wrongs, and are restored in friendship with one another. It is therefore apropos for us to camp out on one of those "r" words next, namely *reconciliation*.

In the chapter above, when thinking about "The Relations*lips* Quiz" question #6, we looked at Matt 5:23–24—which is one of the pantheon passages of Scripture dealing with relational reconciliation (alliteration again

. . . another absolute apology!). Within this text it talks about "be[ing] reconciled" with whomever you are in conflict or disagreement. As I mentioned before when discussing Matt 5, the biblical idea within the word "reconciled" is to change or transform. Like those iconic robotic action figures, the Transformers literally became different creatures when the situation warranted it—from a semi-truck to a planetary defender, and so on. Similarly, when we are offended—and even when we realize we have been the offender toward someone else—God desires for us not to stay the same. We must go through a transformation, or a change, in order to have the relationship be restored again. This is the idea of biblical reconciliation.

And this also is where some who are reading this book will choose to end their interest.

I have heard all the sayings, and know all the mantras, about how generally people are staunchly resistant to change. When the joke starts with "How many Baptists [or Lutherans, or Catholics, or fill-in-your-favorite-group-name-here] does it take to change a light bulb," the punch line is usually something like "Change? What's change?" A good friend has a favorite idiom that is: "I don't like change so much that I don't even keep it in my pocket!" (I know more than a few entrepreneurial children with the same last name as me who would love to be the pal of the person who thinks this way . . . free coins at every point of sale? Cha-ching!) However, without healthy change—the heart kind, not the money kind—nobody will live joyful and sustainable lives.

God causes seasons to change (and there is probably no more evident geographical example of this than my home in Western New York—where lake-effect winter weather storms unleash the likes of "Snowmageddon" one season, and humid heatwaves in the summer cause us as residents to long for wintertime the next). God grows our bodies to change and calls for our minds and habits to follow suit. I remember a conversation with a friend, struggling through Parkinson's Disease, who recounted how defeated he felt that he was now no longer able to fix little things around the house like he once could. This friend was having a difficult time—as I have great compassion for, and understanding for as well—realizing that he had to change his mindset due to the fact that his body was changing (such that he could no longer use a screwdriver to tighten the doorknob in the bathroom). There are many other examples in our lives of how change surrounds us—really *encompasses* us—as if we are being shown by God through the natural world that transformation is a healthy and relevant function of our daily lives. Day to night, and back to day; hunger to satisfaction, only to return to hungry again; our lives are always in a constant state of healthy transformation, and our relationships should be as well.

Especially if we experience relations*lips*—the failure of a healthy relationship—we ought to have our minds and hearts (and likely our pride and behavior as well) rush to the biblical truth of Matt 5:23–24, which is that of transformation. This is the niche of the word "reconciled" which is God's desire for us in our lives together.

So, with that truth of reconciliation and transformation, how can we change—because that is what Jesus says we need to do—in order to make wrong relationships right? Or, how can we change even in our healthy relationships, in order to make ourselves ready and available for new and greater health in the future? The first thing to be prepared for is to get some push-back. You see, Transformers was a cool show and a neat collectible toy series, but the innate notion of change is definitely counter-cultural. Even though change is all around us, society and the human flesh has a presupposition to resist it.

> The world says, in relationships, that when you are brushed off it is okay to *hate*, and to hold *grudges*, and to *bury problems*, and to *not resolve them*, and to *not* forgive.

> But Jesus desires for us to "be reconciled" (Matt 5:24); to *change*.

Change can be as unique as each individual, and as individualized as each unique relational conflict. So, in order to avoid the comprehensiveness of this book reaching the levels of the Encyclopedia Brittanica, I will share with you just a few biblical expectations or examples of how we as people might need to change, with the hopes that the need for change—and the application thereof—will become innately lived out within you. And with each example shared, I intend to also illustrate with a brief story or image that has been helpful to me personally, with the hopes that it might help you to learn just how to be part of the reconciling transformation that Jesus is calling us to.

CHANGE YOUR ACTIONS—

One of the first and most basic principles in our relationships with one another is to *love unconditionally*. Jesus says this in Luke 6:27–28 and 35.

> "But I say to you who hear, love your enemies, do good to those who hate you, bless those who curse you, pray for those who abuse you . . . but love your enemies, and do good, and lend, expecting nothing in return, and your reward will be great, and

you will be sons of the Most High, for he is kind to the ungrateful and the evil."

The hardest thing to live out sometimes is the simplest item in the bunch: *love.* Loving others—especially those who are hard to love—can often be really difficult! So how can we be helped to love others? I believe that Jesus gives us some tips on how to love within the text here: you and I might need to *change our actions.*

Life can often be most simply described as a series of actions. Physics—and ergo the entire physical universe—is simply a series of "action . . . [and] equal and opposite reaction."[1] Human relationships exist because of real and genuine inter*action.* Our structure of communication—such as writing and speaking—hinges not only on pronouns, nouns, adjectives, prepositions, and punctuation, but often most importantly on verbs (many being *action*-verbs). Look at all the actions within these verses:

> It says in verse 27, "*do good* to those who hate you . . . "

> Verse 28 says, "*bless* those who curse you . . . and *pray* for those who spitefully use you."

> And let us not also forget the first action verb in verse 27: "*Love* your enemies . . . " (emphases mine).

Practically speaking, if you are having a hard time loving others, one great biblical exhortation and interpersonal recommendation is to *change your actions* and try doing something that might *assist the love* to come and flood into your heart. That is exactly what these verses in Luke 6 are suggesting. Look, for instance, at the sentence structure of each in another way—and hopefully in a new light:

> Verse 27: "If there are those who hate you, *do good [to them]* . . . "

> Verse 28: "If there are those who curse you, *bless [them]* . . . "

> And again, "If there are those who spitefully use you, *pray for [them]* . . . "

In anticipation of this book, I have written a theological journal article that is a biblical exegetical response to Jesus' words in Luke 6.[2] Within the exegesis—or study and understanding of the truth from within a biblical

1. Isaac Newton's third law of physics.

2. The article, in the *Africanus Journal, Vol. 11 No. 1 (April 2019),* pages five through twelve, which is the biennial scholarly journal of Gordon-Conwell Theological Seminary, is entitled "Relationships *not* Relation*slips*: Life Together Based on Jesus' Words in Luke 6:27–49." A free digital edition of the journal can be found at http://wincc.org/leadership-team/pastor-jason-drapeau/africanus-journal-vol-11-no1.pdf.

text—and further detailed in the journal article, I have mentioned the cultural nuance of *reciprocity*. Simply speaking, reciprocity is the reply of anything concurrent to the situation or scenario at hand (and, yes, being that it is an additional word that starts with the letter "r," it is unfortunately another egregious example of relations*l*ips alliteration!).

An example of reciprocity from my own life and journey is as follows: prior to becoming a pastor and author, I was a public high school teacher. I was incredibly blessed to have been able to teach in a few different schools in a few different states in the U.S. Public education in America is significantly valued in that it is heavily regulated—every teacher, in many (if not all) states, must adhere to certification guidelines in order to maintain, hire and be a teacher in good standing. However, valid teaching certification is dictated at the state level, and not federally. So, as I was a teacher in different school districts in different states, I needed to go through the necessary certification requirements (and sometimes the anecdotally articulated "rigmarole") of transferring my certification from one state to the next.

When I left education as a certified teacher in the state of Pennsylvania and began teaching and subsequently pursuing my teaching certification in the state of Massachusetts, I was hopeful that there would be *reciprocity* between the two states—that the Massachusetts Department of Education would recognize the validity of my teaching certification from the Pennsylvania Department of Education, and be able to "transfer" certification one-for-one without the need to take any additional classes or pass any additional tests.[3] The hope for reciprocity—a like-response based on a likened situation—was the actual vocabulary term used of teacher certification in that setting in public education. However, the term, in any given cultural milieu, can be understood the same way.

In not only the time and setting where the Bible was written, but also in our place and day today, the notion of reciprocity is almost an unspoken expectation:

---

3. If you are curious how my situation turned out, let's just say that I felt incredibly blessed that the Massachusetts Department of Education headquarters was near the city of Boston, MA—which was very close to where I both lived and was to be teaching—because those kind and gracious folks at the MA Department of Education customer service window likely began to know me by name due to all of the times I chose to visit in person, in order to self-advocate for my MA teaching licensure. To make an already long story short, I was eventually able to become a certified licensed teacher in Massachusetts without any student loans or classroom recertification courses, though the cost of gas in city driving to and from their offices the almost innumerable times I paid them visits may have almost been the financial equivalent!

> ▸ If someone greets you on the street with "Hi, how are you," it is appropriately reciprocal[4] to respond with something similar such as "I am fine, and you?"

> ▸ When walking into an establishment with a foyer or vestibule containing two sets of doors, if a person holds open the outside door for you then it is entirely customary for you to reciprocate and likewise hold the inside door open for them.

> ▸ Unfortunately, and negatively as well, if a person cuts you off on the road for no apparent reason whatsoever, it is the engrained human instinct—and the cultural (and innately relationally harmful) reaction of reciprocity—to follow up such rude and disrespectful driving with a diatribe of louder volume, or a hand gesture that frequently only utilizes one particular finger. I cannot condone such action, of course, but some kind of reciprocally rageful response is often innate and tempting by many in that moment!

This same notion of reciprocity can be described to lead and motivate those of Jesus' hearers as he spoke the words in Luke 6. When those in the audience heard Jesus talk about "your enemies . . . those who hate you . . . those who curse you . . . those who abuse you" and so on, their instinctive emotions and desired responses were regarding things that were reciprocal—to similarly *be enemies to them*, and to likewise *hate them*, and to intentionally *curse them*, and to look for ways to relevantly *abuse them*. However, Jesus' actual words, regarding those who perform harm or are antagonistic to us, are words that do *not* affirm reciprocity; they do *not* allow for a response that is the same. Jesus calls for us to *change*, and to be *different* from that which our antagonists are toward us.

A true story that illustrates this so well is as follows: in talking with a friend about God's desires for good and healthy relationships, unprompted he replied with something beautifully complementary. He said, "You know what I do if I have a hard time loving others? I pray for them. Did you know that if you've got a gripe about someone and you pray for them for about 5 minutes a day, then at the end of the week you'll have less frustration and a lot more love than when you started."

How wonderfully confirming is that! This kind of response and reaction to rifts in relationships is exactly the kind of thing that Jesus says we should do: pray for others (see this verbatim in Luke 6:28).

---

4. It is clear to see that "reciprocal" and "reciprocity" have the same root—that of the Latin *reciprocus*, meaning "a returning" (such as "returning like-for-like" or "having a similarly-returned response").

> Not praying spiteful and vindictive things, but rather praying that God mercifully softens their hearts.

> And on the topic of praying for softened hearts, have the next prayer be one that God would soften *your* heart, too!

> Pray that your relationship with them will get better, and that God would make the necessary change in them—and more importantly *in you* as well.

If we follow the advice of my friend, and if we obey the call and command of Jesus to shed reciprocity and instead for us to change, then I suggest that you will be able to almost palpably watch your heart of love grow as you change your actions and attitudes toward others, in order to be ready for a new change of relationship.

CHANGE YOUR VISION—

Another major component to healthy relationships is showing mercy and compassion. See this, as it is coupled along with love, in Luke 6:35–36:

> "But love your enemies, and do good, and lend, expecting nothing in return, and your reward will be great, and you will be sons of the Most High, for he is kind to the ungrateful and the evil. Be merciful, even as your Father is merciful."

While it may be easier to understand the feeling and action of love (hopefully as it has already been described thus far in this book), the understanding of mercy and compassion might be different to grapple with. In order to articulate this, please allow for me to use a personal illustration.

I don't very often have occasions to eat out at restaurants. However, when I do, I feel the joy and calling from God the Holy Spirit to make him known in any way possible—even in leaving a restaurant tip. Many people have a numerical metric for how much they leave for their server at a dining establishment: they give the standard 15–18% or make it a round 20% of the bill. Some people use a simplistic semi-mathematical[5] method, such

---

5. I say "semi-mathematical" because as a former math teacher, I happen to know that most people who simplify their tip-giving as "twice the tax" are actually using that standard as a *cop-out* in order to *avoid* using mental math. Ergo, I cannot condone such actions, since me and mathematics are like peaches and cream. What is most appropriate, mathematically-speaking, is to learn how to calculate round-value percentages when tipping your server—or in any discipline of life, for that matter: a 10% tip is the amount of the bill, while moving the decimal place one digit to the left. 20% is doubling that amount. 15% is half-way between. Goodness gracious, people, it's as simple as

as leaving a tip that is twice the amount of tax on the meal (which I do not recommend, nor condone. See footnote above). Some others still use their tip amount as a meritorious reward for their server's excellence and performance—leaving a larger tip for the employee that worked the hardest and showed the most care and attention, and leaving a lesser tip to the person who was rude and forgetful. In my walk of faith and place of relational maturity, I feel that God has led me to leave every tip as an example of Jesus Christ's *compassionate mercy*. Whether a food worker has delivered exceptional service or not, a larger-than-normal tip accompanied with a "*God* bless you!" hand-written note might just be the kind of pick-me-up that they need for the day, whether deserved or not. In fact, it might speak even more to the character and the soul if a larger tip is left when it is not at all warranted! It can show grace, compassion and mercy on a different level than simple meritorious financial response.

It is very appropriate to have respect—in essence, a measure of love—for any restaurant server. They are people, made in God's image, just like you and I. We are called to love each other, friend and enemy alike. That ought to be universal. However, many people show that they believe that it is alright for further attributes such as compassion and mercy not to be universal, but instead individual. While one person might corral a ladybug in their palm when it is trapped inside the house, showing it compassion and extending mercy to it by bringing it outside and setting it free, another person will not care a thing, or squash it outright with a grunt of "Serves it right, trying to come inside *my* house!" Now, I am not advocating for any specific kind of insect or arachnid rights by using the above example; I am simply sharing that many people do not often initiate unwarranted tender-hearted emotions toward others, or responses of kindness that do not match up with deserved requisite justice (think of our discussion about *reciprocity* above).

In reality, we ourselves are often shown kindness when we don't deserve it, and I find it only fitting that we similarly share total and undeserved kindnesses with others as well. While compassion and mercy might have synonyms like "grace" and "un-merited favor," the idea at its core is that we are able—and in fact are called and commanded by God—to show an elevated and extended demonstration of positive character with others. Truthfully, being compassionate and merciful with others can be hard—especially if others are doing things or saying things that are unjust! After all, it is human instinct to think:

---

drawing a curved arrow underneath a dot on a receipt and multiplying or dividing by two! But, alas, this is a footnote in the section of this book on mercy and compassion, so I must acquiesce . . . however only out of protest (and humor!).

> Where is *my* vindication?

> Where is *my* justice?

I have written a sentiment in earlier chapters that bears repeating: as you are looking *out* at your relationships with others, don't forget to *look up*! If we do so, we may just be reminded that God extends his unmerited favor, kindness, and compassion upon us. God is merciful with you. God is not vengeful with you.

In order to see this—and further, in order to demonstrate this in application to others—I find it helpful to *change our vision*. First, we must change our vision with regards to seeing ourselves in the light of God.

The average American diversifies their life in a number of different ways. When broken down into a typical twenty-four-hour period, people normally spend between five to eight hours a day sleeping. A few hours each day are spent in some sort of bodily maintenance or beautification—from going on walks, to working out in the gym, to bathing and brushing teeth, as well as getting dressed and manicuring one's self in front of a mirror (which, for those of us like myself with a diminishing hairline, are definably less hours than others). Those who have a vocation or calling (either for paid income, or for family support as a caregiver or provision for children or home) usually spend around eight hours each day in such service. There are a few hours daily spent eating food, and even more hours engaged in some kind of visual technology (such as watching T.V., trolling on smartphones and tablets, playing video or computer games, and responding to others via social media on any number of available devices). If you're keeping score at home, that essentially burns through the average person's typical twenty-four-hour day. In my observation and estimation, if there is any time left for demonstrated faith devotion—such as praying or Bible reading—it is typically bequeathed for most people to approximately only 10 minutes of a typical person's daily routine.[6] Ten minutes. Out of an average of 1,440 allotted minutes that each person has in every day, the average American could spend as little as only 10 minutes—the equivalent of less than 0.7% (in other words, *less than one percent*) of their daily chronological allowance on undivided attention to God:

6. As a pastor, I happen to see the most emulatable characteristics of many people—such as in church leadership team meetings, at small group Bible studies, and so on. Even therein, the admission is that daily and substantive spiritual disciplines—like reading Scripture, praying, fasting, spiritual journaling, and so on—are more often difficult and waning, as opposed to vibrant and strong. Couple this with the average non-church attendee, who might never read the Bible and hardly even prays before meals, the average time a person spends with undivided focus and attention toward God is likely and realistically very little.

➤ And then we receive that scary diagnosis from the doctor,

➤ Or we are faced with that financial uncertainty that we weren't prepared for,

➤ Not to mention the relational irritation of others around us that at times seems to be too much for us to bear.

And in *those* very moments, when we cry out to God or are hoping for his benevolence, we somehow expect God to give us *his* undivided attention. All the while, we have the nerve to grow continually frustrated with him when he does not seem to act in exactly the way we are preferring, as if God exists as our "[celestial] maid to bring another pillow to the den."[7]

There are many times when God does, and might, respond with kindness and compassion. In plenty of instances, we ought to receive justice and what is deserved, but instead he shows us mercy. And even if on occasion God does not seem to respond in a way we were hoping—or maybe not even seemingly respond at all—we still would be helped and blessed to have much more of a vertical perspective. If we begin to change our vision, and in a figurative sense "look up," then we can continue in our lives with much greater wisdom and understanding.

In the illustration above, it should be importantly noted that our right response is *not* that we should attempt to *earn* God's favor or try to work before God so that our devotion to God will equal our expectation from him. Plenteous biblical references show clearly that this is not how God operates! In the Bible, Titus 3:5 says, for instance, that God moves not based on our merits, but solely by his own mercy. If we see that—with a change of vision ourselves—it can begin to also influence how we see others.

Additionally, when God calls for us to "be merciful" (Luke 6:36), it is valuable that we understand the reason. If a server at a restaurant gave a guest a dinner mint on a tray, it would not be because they were hungry; on the contrary, dinner mints are given precisely when the guest is full. Oppositely, if a guest was full, the appropriate response would not be to give them a sirloin steak and lobster tail; that is reserved for when the guest is hungry. When a guest is offered steak, or a mint, the context behind it is incredibly telling. So, when God says "be merciful" the reason for mercy is worth pondering.

Why does someone receive compassion and mercy? Precisely because they are *in need of it*. We often times think of people who are mean to us, or who are difficult for us to get along with, as if they are empty shells of a soul—like some kind of evil-filled vessels, beastly monsters, completely

7. Piper, "Prayer: The Work of Missions."

void of anything deserving any mercy or compassion themselves. However, this is normally quite far from the truth. Just like the bully on a playground who picks on other people's insecurities as a defense mechanism in order to deal with his own, so is the case with those who seem to be merciless toward us: in reality, they are prime candidates for needing to be shown mercy themselves.

Every person is the kind of person who needs compassionate mercy—especially those who seem to have no compassion for others at all. That truth bears repeating again itself: those whom you simply cannot stand, because they are cruel and compassionless and mean, are actually the ones who have the most wounded hearts, who themselves need mercy *upon* mercy by you and me in order to be healed. The challenge for us is to change our vision in order to see others differently. Then, I believe, showing mercy to others will come easier for you.

A true personal story might be able to illustrate this. Once, in conversation with someone a number of years ago, our dialogue began to get a bit heated . . . and heated a little more . . . and a little more. After a short period of time, my emotions and the other person's emotions collectively were rising higher and higher until finally the other person had enough and, raising their voice, stormed out of the room. There was now a major rift in our relationship. I had angered the other individual so much that they got in their car and left completely. Not good.

After I had calmed down a bit, and after being given counsel from someone else privy to our conversation, I was convicted to call them up, ask for forgiveness, and try to work on reconciling our relationship. Humbled, I called this person on their cell phone and began by saying that I was sorry for the things that I said which were inappropriate. (Brief sidebar: the things that you have done are the appropriate things to be responsible for. It would not have made the relationship any better by me saying, "Yes, hello? I would like to begin by pointing out your faults in our conversation and demanding that you apologize." I'd like to see *any* relationship improve with others-focused language like that! Rather, the value in reconciliation is recognizing that *you* are responsible for whatever *you* have brought to the table, no matter how irrelevant it is in comparison. Further, the responsibility continues with me to forgive others regardless of whether they are sorry or say so, just as it is on me to say that I am sorry for my wrongs—and actually *be* sorry in order to work on making the relationship right.)

So that is what I did: I already had forgiven this person for their role in the heated conversation, and I never brought up, nor expected, their reciprocal request for forgiveness. And I said that I was sorry, that I wanted to work on making our relationship better, and I concluded with the oft-familiar good-mannered phrase, "Would you please forgive me?" And the person's response was sharp and biting and just as surprising, as they said with a stern tone, "Forgiveness isn't something you ask for; it's something you just throw out there, and you don't expect anything in return!"

In that very moment, God the Holy Spirit gave me a change of vision in how I saw this person. I began to see them instantaneously in a compassionate and merciful way. It was as if scales fell from my eyes, and I was aware of this person in a brand new light: I saw the individual not as someone who had just hurt me—even though that was the case—but instead as a wounded and hurting and mercy-needing bruised soul themselves. What I saw, in that moment, based on what was said to me—when the person barked harshly and incorrectly that their expectation was about forgiveness being something that people are supposed to just *throw out there* and *never expect in return*—is that this person had possibly never truly forgiven anyone. In fact, it is possible that this individual had never truly experienced genuine forgiveness by others as well.

It was as if I could envision the person being bruised, and battered, and abused, and insulted, and hurt again and again in the past, all the while holding on to memoirs of others' offenses, one after another, after another, after another. I could picture the person with an overflowing pile of reminders of the pain that people had caused, with no outlet to let that pain go. Further, even if any of the individual attackers happened to have good manners and wielded the idea of sorrow, I could picture a kind of faux forgiveness being doled their way—as if the offenders just threw shoddy "sorry's" and fake apologies out there in the past. My vision was changed, and I could now see that this person was holding on to these things like *hurt receipts*. I was asking: "Will you forgive me? Will you allow for me to take that hurt away, so that the wound is a little bit less, and so that our relationship can grow a little bit more?" Yet they were unable to part with the hurt receipt that I had caused and given . . . and they were holding on to a whole bunch more from the past as well.

Even now to this day, I see this person not as the bully, or the bruiser, or the wounder that they sometimes might be. I see the individual as the hurting, and the needy, and the bruised, and the wounded.

Because I had a change of vision, I can now see that the individual is the kind of person who needs mercy. If you similarly change your vision, then you just might be able to see those who hurt you as being the very kind of people who are holding on to past hurts themselves. And maybe you'll be able to show compassion and kindness and mercy to them like you never thought before.

CHANGE YOUR MEMORY—

Probably one of the biggest components to being ready for healthy relationships is forgiveness. Jesus says that we need to forgive. This is clear in many places in the Bible, one being Luke 6:37:

> "Judge not, and you will not be judged; condemn not, and you will not be condemned; forgive, and you will be forgiven."

Such a huge part of forgiveness is another word that begins with the same letter. You might have heard them go together: the word pairing is *"forgive* and *forget."* One reason, I believe, that so many people have a hard time forgiving each other is because they are unwilling to forget the sins and wrongs that others have done against them.

> - "Can you believe what that person posted on Facebook *an hour ago . . .* "
> - "Well, *a week ago*, they said this to me, which was pretty ignorant for them to say . . . "
> - "I'm not going to the family party, because, well, you remember what happened *a year ago . . .* "
> - "What they did to me *ten years ago* was just so wrong . . . "

Something that flies in the face of the mind's most indelible memory of our hurts is yet the most profound, complex, spiritual, theological, and relational truth: *let it go*. It never fails to amaze me that the most deep and rich and desperately needed fact is often the most short and sweet. If you would like your relationships to improve, then regarding the wrongs against you that others have done, you simply need to let things go. God speaks this very truth from his own Word, in Isa 43:25, when he says:

> "I, I am he who blots out your transgressions for my own sake, and I will not remember your sins . . . "

God not remembering our sins? Is this even possible? If we wonder whether God possibly spoke in error, he helps us out by not only reiterating this again in Jer 31:34, but also doubling-down with forgiveness:

> "For I will forgive their iniquity, and I will remember their sin no more."

God—even God—who knows all things, willingly chooses to forget our sins, for those who trust in his name. Not only does God not remember our sin, but the link between this "forgetting" and God "forgiving" is evident in Heb 10:17–18:

"Then [God] adds, '*I will remember their sins and their lawless deeds no more.*' Where there is *forgiveness of these*, there is no longer any offering for sin" (emphasis mine).

Now I know that this could bring up a theological quandary regarding the divine. "How in the world can an omniscient—an all-knowing—God somehow forget? That is seemingly inconsistent, or at least incompatible, with his limitless knowledge!" I definitely understand the argument. So please allow for me to explain it in this way: God, in his omniscience, with regards to the sins of those who are forgiven followers of him, *chooses not to bring them back up in his mind.*

Undoubtedly anthropomorphic analogies[8] regarding God fall short. We are trying to illustrate or understand the divine with our mortal minds and imperfect words. Similarly, we may feel that there are such massively consequential sins or egregious wrongs committed against us that are seemingly impossible to forget. I was just recently reminded, yet again, of the horrific enduring memory of many kinds of abuse and offense, as one sexual assault survivor described to the courtroom during a rape trial that she herself was "serving a life sentence in recovery" because of the memory of the trauma she experienced from her assailant.[9] For some people—and because of the magnitude of the wrongs done against us—simply choosing to not recall things to memory can be an incredibly difficult ordeal. I am by no means undermining or delegitimizing the gravity of depravity. It is often very difficult to forget.

With regard to other people's sins, many of us have a better memory than God . . . and this is nothing commendable whatsoever.

———— ∫ ————

8. The idea of an anthropomorphism is giving human attributes to something—or someone—that is not human. My saying that God does not bring our sins to mind is a frail illustration, because God does not have a "mind" or a "brain" like humans have minds or brains. However, the idea is still the same; with regards to eternal judgment, for those who have personal faith in Jesus Christ, all of our sins are exchanged for the sinless righteousness of Jesus Christ, because Jesus bore our sins upon his death on the cross. Therefore, for all who rely upon Jesus for their salvation, God is not mindful of our sin— he is instead aware of the sacrifice of his Son for our eternal destiny. Thanks be to God!

9. Grinberg, "A former UK officer was convicted of rape on a Tinder date, but his victim says trauma is a 'life sentence.'"

All the same, if an all-knowing God chooses not to bring our sins to mind when thinking of us—our transgressions against him that are egregious and likely ten thousand times more frequent or more severe than the occasional offense of others against us—then there just may still be hope for us to change our memories and choose not to bring up others' wrongs. If we desire to walk in right relationships, you must change your memory—synonymously, *let it go*, and in some kind of way choose to *forget*.

I have found it to be a very stark truth, and a very impactful statement, to share with those whom I often counsel: that with regard to other people's sins, *many of us have a better memory than God* . . . and this is *nothing* commendable whatsoever. Often our relationships are worsened as a result.

A story that illustrates the power of changing your memory is as follows: a husband and wife came in to see a counselor because they were having problems in their marital relationship. They each had their specific things to say to the counselor, but it became apparent during the counseling session that in this particular case, the husband was much more embittered and full of gripes. "My wife always does *this*, and it just drives me crazy . . . and then she does *that*, and it drives me crazy even more!" On and on he went, bringing up seemingly every detail of his wife's past errors and flaws.

The counselor, at the end of the session, gave the couple an assignment to do at home. "I want you to each get a jar—like a sugar canister or a cookie dish—and I want you to write down, on little slips of paper, whatever the other person does that upsets you throughout the week. Write them down when they occur, one offense at a time, and put each of them in your jar. Next week we'll open the jars and talk about it."

So that week, the husband and wife each got their own jar. And during the week, the husband was fervently jotting down things whenever his wife did something that irked him, stuffing his jar full. At the end of the week, they came back together with the counselor, the husband's jar overflowing with things that *he vividly remembered* and wrote down that his wife did to upset him that week. Before the counselor, and with a scowl toward his wife, the man seemed to thoroughly enjoy sharing every single scrap page. When it was the wife's turn, she took her jar, opened it up, and pulled out only one single piece of paper from inside. What she had written were these simple words: "I love you."

In this story, without any hesitation, it is clear who was the one ready to forgive. It was the wife, who chose to only exercise her memory positively, and to exclusively recall love over and above her husband's wrongs. You see, the husband himself was not above reproach, and was not a perfect person or free from any flaws. I can just about relate to that presumption myself, as I am sure that one of these days, I will eventually do something that will frustrate my wife. (Similar to how I can almost guarantee the hearty laugh that all wives would have in reading such a joke as this!) Husbands are not perfect; rather, the wife in this story had chosen to forget. She had changed her memory and was ready for the relationship to be healed and full of forgiveness and love.

We can't change other people; only God can do that. We can't even necessarily change our relationships, especially if the other person is unwilling to reconcile and make the relationship right. But we *can change ourselves.* And in doing so, we can be ready for the healthy relationships that God has in store for us. Remember: you, yourself, are exactly half of the people involved in all of the relationships you have in your life (because relationships involve someone else *and you*).

In order to have and maintain healthy relationships, God is calling for you to *change your actions,* and pray for those who you have a hard relationship with. God calls for you to *change your vision* and see those who are hard to get along with as being people who are hurting and who need God's mercy. You are called to follow after God and *change your memory,* and forget what others have done to you, in order to begin to forgive and get ready for the relationship to be right.

There are, for sure, a thousand other practical tips from Jesus' mouth, from God's Word, and from the Holy Spirit's prompting, all of which can help to make us ready to have right relationships with others. We would be right to follow all of them. The reason that God cares so much about right relationships, and the reason that we should be all about it ourselves as well, is because God went to great extremes to make our relationship with him right for all time. Truthfully, there was nothing that God had done to cause our relationship with him to be marred in the first place! He is utmost in perfection and brilliant in excellency. It was us, in our sin, in our wrongs, who needed to become pure and right in order to be with God.

All the same, there is nothing good that we have done, or can still do, that will be enough change for a right relationship with God on our own. So Jesus went through everything on our behalf for us to be reconciled to God; when he died on that cross, Jesus made a way for you and God to be right. Oh, that we would not just believe on this and thank him, but that we would also try to live rightly with one another as well, out of obedience and gratitude to God.

Chapter 5

—— ∫ ——

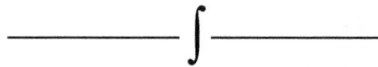

Relations*l*ip Objections

JESUS HAS MUCH TO say about our relationships with others. In the Bible, Luke 6 has given us a great framework of how to approach health with one another. Further, the barren ground of our unhealthy relationships—and our own unhealthy habits within those relationships—has given plenty of real-world examples of the need for relational reconciliation, as well as the ability and necessity by which to practice it in our lives together.

But in our understanding and awareness of need, we have thus far missed one very important thing: objections.

> ➤ Some of you might have some serious objections to what has been written and suggested thus far, possibly thinking that healthy relational habits are unnecessary or unwarranted in certain circumstances.

> ➤ Some of you might have some questions about certain relational situations that you think the Bible is particularly irrelevant about.

Objections and questions are important and fair, and valuable to be addressed. I encourage you, however, to humbly approach a question or objection with an open mind to change—just as what was last stated in the previous chapter above—and strive to be free from your own presuppositions. It would not be helpful to have this frame of reference, for example: "Before anybody responds to me, I am deciding in advance that I'm right, and no response or answer by Jesus or the Bible or this paltry book's author can prove me wrong; I'm just going to boastfully air my objections as justification for why I believe it is okay to treat others like trash and leave damaged relationships unrestored." If that is your preferred posture, then you are candidly attempting to defy relational gravity; it simply will not work and is not authentic or correct. Approaching this book—namely, approaching Jesus' words in Scripture that I am restating in the context of this book—with an air of prideful irreconciliatory presuppositions is at best disingenuous, and at worst dangerous. It certainly may be your prerogative to have such a position, but it is not in the least beneficial. In the words of one of my former seminary professors: "It's okay to disagree with me; *you can be wrong.*"

All humor and levity aside, what we have been looking at thus far regarding healthy relationships are not my own ideologies or recommendations. Although they may be phrased within my own particular voice, it is helpful to remember that the ground of this book is the text of the Bible, God's Word. As a result, my quoting Scripture and restating its principles are definitely not my words or ideas about relationships; they are *God's*. Many of that which has been shared in the chapters and pages above, and in those to come as well, are words recorded as coming straight from Jesus' mouth (such as what we have seen in Luke 6), and because of such divine ethos, these words should be followed without disagreement or challenge. All the same, I understand that there still might be a few objections—or scenarios or questions—that are worth our time and attention on the topic. So, let us look at a few of those objections now.

One objection to the need and importance of healthy relational reconciliation is the thought that we ought to be able to treat others differently, and that people are not required to like everyone else in the same way. Isn't it an instinctive natural reaction to enjoy one person better than another? Why can't we embrace others based on our own preferences, likenesses, and treatments? Can't we just treat others based on how they treat us?

Truthfully it is easy to love those whom we like to love, and it is similarly hard to love those whom are hard for us to love. Especially in the Christian community, we are exceptionally good at using religiously nuanced words to justify and rationalize our distance from others. Sure, it sounds noble when we use phrases like "I am just *guarding my heart* from this person," or "It is important to *protect my peace*, and *shelter my soul*." Quite simply, these phrases are hogwash wrapped in holiness. They sound nice, but in reality, they are simply veneers hiding judgmentalism and relational prejudice.

Jesus himself actually anticipates this kind of objection specifically . . . and he doesn't buy it. In fact, he challenges us that we are to love all, and all the same. See what Jesus says specifically in Luke 6:32–33.

> "If you love those who love you, what benefit is that to you? For even sinners love those who love them. And if you do good to those who do good to you, what benefit is that to you? For even sinners do the same."

In this text, Jesus is essentially saying that if you only love those whom you love to love, then you are no better than a pagan sinner. This kind of "like-for-like" perspective is exactly the construct of reciprocity that has been mentioned earlier. Further, as it is a significant enough repetition to be warranted, let's all be reminded once again that in our relationships and interactions with others, as you are looking around at each other, *don't forget to look up.*

Imagine for a moment if God had the same kind of limited, conditional, love-only-if-loved-in-return kind of love for you. If God only responded to you based upon the merit of how you responded to him first. If God only bestowed upon you the level of prioritization as to how often, in your day, you prioritized him. Not sure about the rest of you, but I'd be a goner—there could possibly be an *ant* that has more respect and admiration for God on some days than this humble author! (It is important to note that I am not proud of this the least as well.)

The reality is that God does not withhold his affection for us in collateral for our affection toward him. Instead, God's love for you is unbalanced and unconditional—he loves you no matter what you do. Certainly, God desires for our love toward him to grow and not remain stagnant, of course, just as he also desires that we not live rebelliously and take for granted the love that he has for us. But God is the Divine Initiator, loving us despite our frailty and apathy toward him. This is most beautifully seen in Rom 5:8, which says:

> " . . . but God shows his love for us in that while we were still sinners, Christ died for us . . . "

If Jesus only had conditional love for us, and if Jesus only loved those whom he loved to love, then it is very possible that he would never have loved—nor shown his love—for you. Humbly, there are a thousand days in your lifetime when you have not cared a thing about loving Jesus, or showing him your love. But God's Word says that in spite of how we act toward him, God still and instead, through Jesus Christ, loves us.

God models this behavior for us, toward us. We can love others as well, even if they don't love us back, or even if they are not like us and are difficult to love. We are able to demonstrate this to others because, frankly, that's exactly what Jesus does to us. Further, it is reliance upon God the Holy Spirit in order for us to love those who are difficult to love. The instincts and unctions required to treat others nicely who are not nice to us is evident in the words of Alfred Plummer, who wrote, "To return evil for good is devilish; to return good for good is human; to return good for evil is divine."[1]

The prevailing principles of healthy relationships
. . . are always to govern and structure whatever
boundaries that you set in your lives.

∫

It would be valuable at this time to share that I understand appropriate and beneficial boundaries that can be set within relationships, in order to work at keeping our relationships continually healthy in the long run. For example, if you have an axe murderer as your roommate—which is a questionable move at best, but stay with me—and one afternoon they, shall we say, aggressively approach you to high-five your face with an implement of choice, then we are commanded to still *love them* . . . but yes, I think you are also okay to lovingly encourage them to find another place to live (or decide to move out yourself). More sincerely, if a friend or co-worker is regularly abusive in some other way relationally, then we are commanded by Jesus to still *love them* . . . but yes, I think it is also okay to not feel like we need to hang out with them all the time. There are plenty of people whom God calls for me to love that I am likewise discerned to never allow for them to babysit my children because of their actions or their character, for instance. But am I ever justified to stop loving them? The answer is always and unequivocally *no*, because the heart behind everything is to be Jesus Christ's love.

The prevailing principles of healthy relationships—such as unconditional love, forgiveness, and so on—are always to govern and structure whatever boundaries that you set in your lives. You should never send someone away or keep somebody apart from you out of spite, or anger, or because of your remembrance of their sin. On the contrary, God forgives

---

1. Plummer, *An Exegetical Commentary on the Gospel According to St. Matthew*, 89.

and forgets your sin—and mine. So, you, too, need to change your memory, and forgive and forget and let go of others' wrongs, too—even in establishing healthy boundaries with others. Nowhere in Jesus' teaching do we see that we are justified to only love those who love us. In fact, Luke 6:32–33 shows that objection being thrown right out the window.

Another objection to keeping relationships right is when we think that others' offenses or sins are too bad, or that they are too fresh in our minds for us to be able to move forward with reconciling a relationship. "Listen, pastor/author/relational-reconciler-guy, I hear you say that we need to love and forgive and make peace and all that stuff. But you have no idea what they said to me! You have no clue just how much they hurt me! What they did was so bad that I can just never forgive them for it."

In only one respect, that objection may be right: there is the possibility that I, myself, as just one person, might not know what so-and-so said to you, or how much they hurt you, or what they did to you. There is no way that I can claim to have gone through the kind of hurt and sin and relational damage that everyone has gone through. On the other hand, pastors and authors are people, too. And this guy *does* especially happen to be someone who many, many people have hurt throughout the years. My character has been assassinated; my family has been humiliated; my job significance has been questioned; and all, candidly, without a single ounce of warrant. At the onset, please don't be too quick to assume that I have lived on an island of tranquility my whole life. The reality is that I've been bludgeoned by quite a few branches after falling down the relations*l*ips tree. So, I might actually be able to understand some of the hurts that many of you have gone through, and I am still passionately pursuing right relationships and purposefully commissioned by God to call you to reconciliation as well.

However, my ethos is not even the greatest rebuttal to that objection—and that objection does have a significant need to be rebuffed. This is a much more significant response instead:

> Jesus Christ, the eternally-begotten Son of God, is the One who knows exactly every single one of your hurts, because he paid for each and every one of them when he died on the cross. And, he is the omniscient, forever-existing creator of the universe, and still said that we should walk in healthy relationships with God and one another all the same.

The statement above might be a bit difficult to understand at the onset and is significantly a macro-level response to a micro-personal and individual objection. Therefore, I humbly ask over the next few paragraphs, that you do your best to track with me.

Which events of life came more recently: Jesus' words in Luke 6 about relationships—such as to love and to forgive and to show mercy and to reconcile—or *your hurts* that someone else committed against you? Again, which is the newer item in the timeline of history: what Jesus said some 2000 years ago, as we have recorded in the Bible, or your hurt which was done to you one hour ago, or one day ago, or one week ago, or one year ago? What many people would believe—even most of you reading at this moment—is that you would contend that what Jesus spoke some 2000 years ago came *first* (as it was the older event), and the hurts that others did to us came more *recently* (as being more fresh and new).

However, that is actually incorrect. The *"older"* item is the hurt that we have experienced; the *"newer"* thing is actually what Jesus says.

Confused? Lost? Please allow for me to explain.

You see, many people think that the timeline of history contains an order something like this:

1. Jesus came to earth some 2000 years ago,

2. Soon after, Jesus said what he said about relationships and other things,

3. Then thousands of years passed, until you arrived on the scene,

4. And then someone said something, or did something, against you,

5. To which you were soon thereafter deeply hurt by it,

6. And that brings us to the present moment in the present day.

But the reality is—even though difficult to understand—this is exactly backwards. You see, Jesus wasn't simply just some historical figure who lived and spoke 2000 years ago. Jesus is God. He is eternal and forever. Look at these words from Col 1:15–17.

> "He [Jesus Christ] is the image of the invisible God, the firstborn of all creation. For by him all things were created, in heaven and on earth, visible and invisible, whether thrones or dominions or rulers or authorities—all things were created through him and for him. And he is before all things, and in him all things hold together."

Some of you reading this might seek to call my bluff, saying, "Look, Buddy, your theological gymnastics don't hold suit. This says itself that Jesus 'is before all things.' See? I told you that Jesus came first, then my hurts came more recently. What kind of nonsense are you talking about!" Granted, I understand your reading of these verses. However, that is not this text's intent. Jesus is God, and is eternal. The first *and the last*. From beginning *to end*.

The very same verse here that says "he is before all things" also ends with "in him all things hold together." You can't hold something together unless that thing is at its created culmination, being fully crafted and completed. In other words, Jesus exists at the start, and at the finish. He is still holding together all things—past-occurring, presently-existing, future-arriving—and he is eternally-relevant and currently speaking through his Word, the Bible.

Jesus was there when the world began, and Jesus is in heaven now awaiting his return at this world's approaching end. The Triune Godhead is truly everlasting, as it says elsewhere in Scripture—such as Isa 46:8–10, for instance:

> "Remember this and stand firm, recall it to mind, you trans-gressors, remember the former things of old; for I am God, and there is no other; I am God, and there is none like me, declaring the end from the beginning and from ancient times things not yet done, saying, 'my counsel shall stand, and I will accomplish all my purpose.'"

Jesus is God, not just some guy 2000 years ago who said a few things that were written down in a dusty book. Jesus sees history from the future back. Jesus sees every hurt, and pain, and broken relationship, and spiteful word, and terrible deed done against you, and done by you. As part of God's plan, Jesus still came to earth 2000 years ago, and he still said what he said, and it was still recorded in God's Word, even though he knew exactly what they said about you, or said to you, or did against you. I know that it is difficult to wrap our chronologically-minded thoughts around it, but the fact is that in the realm of eternity, Jesus saw all the hurts that would be done against you in our present and future *first* . . . and he *still* spoke his words in his Word, calling for you and I to show unconditional love and forgiveness.

Many people might couple their hurts with more objections to Jesus' words about relational reconciliation, thinking that what Jesus says[2] is out-dated and irrelevant compared to the more current and terrible hurt that has gone on in our lives:

2. Even the blend of verb tenses throughout this book are careful and intentional, as best as I am able to tell, so as to describe and illustrate the *past* nature of our hurts, compared to the *presently*-relevant words and commands of Jesus to reconcile and restore relationships and forgive others. It is historically accurate that as Jesus lived and walked and spoke some 2000 years ago, the past tense verb or phrase "Jesus said" would be grammatically authentic in the footnote mention above. However, as I have written in the sentence in which this footnote is linked, I have not described "what Jesus *said*" (in history), but rather that "Jesus *says*"—in the *present tense*. This is because as explained in this chapter, the truth is that through the Bible, God's Word, Jesus is still speaking; he is still presently calling us to healthy relationships in the present and future day, no matter what has occurred to us in the past.

> ➤ As if God's plan was archaic when Jesus said those words 2000 years ago,

> ➤ And then when we are hurt today, we say "Yeah, but God, that person said and did these things to me . . . "

> ➤ Presuming all the while that God's response in our present day would be, "Oh my . . . hmmm . . . I didn't anticipate *that* happening to you! Alright, well, let's change my Word. You're okay not to love them, and not to forgive them, and to keep living your life with resentment against them. What that person did was fresh enough and bad enough for you to hold a grudge against them. That's fine."

Jesus doesn't resound from heaven when someone offends you, saying, "Attention, everyone! Scratch out the words of my Book. That thing that just happened 10 seconds ago was so new and so bad that it doesn't apply to my old words anymore. Being grouchy is now okay." Because Jesus is God, he sees and speaks in time from the future back. He knows intimately and eternally and exactly what you are going through, and he *still* says what he said. Jesus hears precisely what people say about you and he *still* says what he said. Jesus knows personally the hurt and pain that others put you through, and he *still* says what he said. Jesus not only sees what someone posted on Facebook about you, but he even sees into their heart and knows why they did it, and he *still* says what he said. Jesus' words to love, forgive, and reconcile are never trumped by what has been done to you, no matter how often or recent or egregious. Jesus still says it. The challenge is great, but it is a challenge all the same: not to object, but rather to abide by it.

As if the Son of God's eternal omniscience (all-knowingness) wasn't enough credibility, Jesus Christ—when living on this earth—went through the world's most gruesome hurt himself, when he was:

1. Betrayed by his closest friends,

2. Called a liar (even though he was perfectly true),

3. Convicted of crimes he never committed,

4. Beaten by his countrymen and foreigners alike,

5. Mocked and made fun of by citizens and passers-by,

6. Required to endure physical torture,

7. And finally, crucified on a cross, and died with no earthly justice.

Yes, Jesus knows exactly the kinds of hurts, offenses, and sins committed by others against you. In fact, since none of us reading this book have ever succumbed to arguably the most excruciating form of execution in the history of the world, namely death on a cross (to such an extent that the term "excruciating" has at its root the word "crucifixion" by likeness to somehow describe its gruesomeness), we can safely say that whatever we have gone through, as difficult as it may have been, all the same pales in comparison to the enduring sufferings of the Son of God. All the while, in full knowledge of the impending cross, regarding the words from Luke 6 about relational health and reconciliation Jesus still said this: he still said to love, and to forgive, and to make peace. In fact, while hanging on that very cross, Jesus responded in this way, with these very words coming from Jesus' own lips:

> "And when they came to the place that is called The Skull, there
> they crucified him . . . And Jesus said, '*Father, forgive them*, for
> they know not what they do'" (Luke 23:33–34, emphasis mine).

Forgiveness is difficult, indeed. Even hearing about Jesus declaring forgiveness for the very people who put him on the cross might not crack the hard shell of your heart when it comes to forgiving other people who have virulently offended you. However, the consequences of unforgiveness can be even more deadly. The playwright Michael Christopher penned a dramatization entitled *The Black Angel* in which a Nazi German general named Herman Engel was put on trial for, among other things, the massacre of the family of Morrieaux, a French journalist. Engel was sentenced to thirty years' imprisonment by the Nuremberg Court, which led to a furious Morrieaux plotting to take Engel's life upon his release. You see, Morrieaux not only thought Engel should be executed for killing his entire family, but he also spent every day of Engel's imprisonment enacting deadly retribution of the general in his own heart.

After Engel's release as a frail old man, Morrieaux finally made good on his plan. Stirring up the nearby villagers to shoot the former Nazi general and burn his residence to the ground the next day, Morrieaux decided to visit the now elderly man the night before his impending death. What he found was not a savage wartime leader, but a broken and humbled soul, living out his final days before he passed away from old age. Feeling moved with compassion, Morrieaux 'fessed up' and shared with Engel the murderous scheme that was planned for him the following eve. Morrieaux was willing to help the old general escape but was frozen when Engel shared these words: "I will flee with you, but only if you will forgive me." A compassionate Morrieaux was glad to help an old man escape a vengeful mob, but to forgive him in his heart was something that he found too difficult to do. Morrieaux simply could not bring himself to forgive, and so Engel chose to stay, where the next day he succumbed to death at the hands of the Frenchman's malefactors.[3]

Forgiveness is indeed a difficult discipline, but it is far better than being disciplined by God or our own sorrowful and calloused conscience when feeling seemingly unable to forgive. The reality is that there is nothing too bad, or too fresh and new, that cannot be forgiven and loved through. Jesus' Word is present and current even still, and says that we are to extend forgiveness and pursue right relationships through it all.

Another objection comes from a place of fear regarding relational reconciliation. "I try to avoid confrontation, and this seems like it's too hard to make this relationship right—plus, I don't want to get into another fight with them. I think I'll just avoid them, and let time pass." A few encouragements regarding this objection and ideology come as follows: first, it is important to note that "timidness" is not one of the fruits of the Spirit that God desires for us to emulate (see Gal 5:22–23). We are to be bold and brave, even if it means that in doing so we must also become uncomfortable. Thankfully, Jesus Christ was not timid when it came time for him to reconcile our relationship with God by means of dying on the cross. Jesus became wonderfully brave and strong, in the face of conflict and adversity and confrontation, and it has allowed for all who trust in him by faith to have a right-standing relationship with God for eternity. Thanks be to God!

Jesus' strength and courage comes across through a true story: I recall hearing of a young man who begrudgingly attended a church worship service one evening. He was raised in the setting and culture of thinking that in order to be tough, you had to show yourself as strong by force. To him and many other young men the same, Jesus came across as a softie because he didn't stand up for himself but instead "rolled over" and let his opponents kill him. That seemed, to this young man, to be weak. On the street, if someone fronts you, you'd take them down; show them who's boss. And so, in this church, with the preacher mindful of his audience, this young man heard words that were counter-cultural to his thoughts on the Savior. "Don't none of y'all be callin' my Jesus no punk," the preacher said. He went on to describe the incredible toughness and grit that it took to sustain lashings, beatings, starvation, and the grueling endurance of the cross. Jesus' body and will was not weak, the preacher claimed; Jesus was *strong*. It took precisely that kind of strength—fully reliant upon God the Father—for Jesus who "endured the cross" (Heb 12:2) to make our relationship with God

---

3. As recounted by Lewis B. Smedes in *Forgive and Forget*, 24–25.

right.[4] We are likewise called to endure any kind of discomfort, through God's strength, so that our relationships with others may be right likewise.

Another response to the objection of fear and timidity is an important restatement of that which was brought up in the Relations*l*ips Quiz question #5 in chapters earlier; namely, that "time heals all wounds" is *not* a quote from Jesus, and is in fact precisely *un-biblical*. In this sense, cowardice is the father of apathy. What we are apprehensive in doing is precisely what we are more than likely never willing to do. Instead of our apprehension, God calls for us to have bold and biblical conviction in order to make relationships right. Simply letting time pass with the hopes that our relationships will get better (really, with the motive that we are too nervous or cowardly to do the hard work in restoring friendships) will ultimately lead to social scars within both us and others. The outcome of nervous inaction is nothing beneficial, but in fact will lead to further separation and lessened relational health.

As a pastor, I have had the privilege—and experienced the harrowing and humbling reality—of ministering to those who are on their deathbed. For some, the time in contemplation and prayer with patient and family during a person's final days is incredibly rewarding. For others, it is gut-wrenching and sad. In my hospital visits and chaplaincy ministry, I have unfortunately had difficult visits with patients on the verge of death from a number of things, but none is more depressing than cirrhosis of the liver. This gruesome condition can realistically come through a few different means, but is most prevalent as a result of alcoholism and irreparable damage done to the body because of unending alcohol abuse.

The human body processes stiff drink—especially constant over-use of it—through the liver, where each abuse actually injures and scars this vital organ. The damage done eventually heals, but with scar tissue replacing, and instead of, healthy vibrant liver cells. Think of receiving a bad cut to the skin from a saw or rough serrated blade, requiring jagged stitches at the site of the wound; the injury will eventually heal, but the restored scar tissue will always be more sensitive and prone to skin cancers, the formation of keloids, and further injury. Cirrhosis is somewhat similar to this, but with one of the body's most vital internal organs—and thereby with many more significant repercussions if damaged. Over constant alcohol abuse, and after a period of time, healthy liver cells are replaced with essentially dead liver scar tissue, rendering this vital organ next to impossible to function. A patient who is dying of cirrhosis of the liver becomes a shell of their former self; withered, weakened, and dying without any remedy for recovery.

4. It was exactly this kind of message—showing Jesus Christ in enduring the cross *as* strong—that God chose to use in order to lead the young man in this church service to a relationship with him.

I have stood by those hospital beds—especially after sitting in counseling sessions with the same healthy individual months' prior, encouraging them to seek treatment from addiction and be free from the throes of their struggles with alcohol before it kills them. It has been painful and incredibly sad to watch death from cirrhosis, knowing that there could have been healthy cells and a healthy life lived instead, if other better decisions were made earlier. With regards to letting tension lay in relationships, the same "cirrhosis of the friendship" will unhealthily scar both people, preventing other healthy relationships from forming in the future, and eventually leading to a lack of vibrant life for any interpersonal interaction. The greater need is to not let time pass, but instead to carry the mantle of bold and brave reconciliation, lest our hearts and emotions die in the meantime.

The concern of fear is also not one that Jesus leaves unaddressed. God is powerfully present and available for us in all cases, especially in walking the road of right relationships. In fact, one of the most misquoted verses in all of the Bible shows this to be beautifully true.

Many Christians, especially church-attending and prayer-meeting participants, will often be quick to memorize or recite that "where two or three are gathered in my name, there am I among them" (Matt 18:20). It is quoted in the middle of a worship service or during a small group time of prayer, such as: "Dear God, we are praying here as a group of two or three or more, and as your Word says, 'Where two or three are gathered,' we acknowledge that you are here with us, oh Lord." Although that may be true—that God is with us wherever we go—this passage of Scripture is not the appropriate context for that quotation.[5] Rather, "where two or three are gathered in my name" is actually a quotation of the emboldening and encouraging presence of Jesus *in the midst of relational reconciliation.*

The larger context that gives evidence to this is Matt 18:15–20, which is as follows:

> "If your brother sins against you, go and tell him his fault, between you and him alone. If he listens to you, you have gained your brother. But if he does not listen, take *one or two others* along with you, that *every charge may be established by the evidence of two or three witnesses.*[6] If he refuses to listen to them, tell

5. Other more appropriate and more contextually-accurate evidences in the Bible that God is with us would be Scriptures pointing to God's omnipresence (such as Ps 139:7–10; Jer 23:23–24; Acts 17:27–28), as well, of course, as the incarnation of God the Son, Jesus, who was also called "Immanuel," meaning "God [is] with us" (see Isa 7:10–8:10; Matt 1:18–25).

6. This italicized sentence portion is a quotation from Deut 19:15, also within a greater context of legal and relational matters (brought on by sin) in the community

it to the church. And if he refuses to listen even to the church, let him be to you as a Gentile and a tax collector. Truly, I say to you, whatever you bind on earth shall be bound in heaven, and whatever you loose on earth shall be loosed in heaven. Again I say to you, *if two of you agree on earth* about anything they ask, it will be done for them by my Father in heaven. *For where two or three are gathered in my name*, there am I among them" (emphasis mine).

This passage is often referred to as "church discipline," because it is a sort of script for keeping purity and righteousness within the church of God. However, it is important to notice that the aim of this passage is not reprimand nor corporate excommunication; in fact, that is the *least*-desired outcome and the absolute last resort! The second sentence within the first verse of this passage states that the hope is for "you [to] have gained your brother." The goal of the church, just the same as the goal of each of us individually as well, is to have right relationships *one to another* (in fact, that is how this restorative process begins: as seen in the first part of verse 15, where we are to meet " . . . between you and him [or her as well, by context] alone . . . "). Meeting with someone with whom there is disharmony is meant to be done boldly and courageously, one on one, so that you may each regain harmony with one other, in the brotherhood and sisterhood of healthy unity.

Part of the objection of fear comes when our minds extrapolate the negative outcomes of a situation. Nobody would rightly be fearful if, when a relationship is severed, we imagine a glorious remedy: "Hey, I bet if I ask to get together for coffee with them, they'll say yes, and we'll sit and really listen humbly to each other, forgive one another, and become really good friends afterward as a result!" Timidity does not become king in that thought process. However, our minds generally imagine the worst possible scenario: more yelling, more humiliating, more tension, worse feelings, and a worsened relationship *after* the attempt than before it. God is not aloof to our tendency toward thinking cataclysmic thoughts such as this, nor to a distinct harsh and plausibly difficult unintentional end (as any relationship between two sinfully flawed individuals has at least a non-zero probability of turning due south in no time). God's desire for us all the same is to not *dwell* upon a sour outcome or *presume* it as becoming likely. He reminds us that in the process of restoring any difficult relationship, *he is there with us*

---

of Israel. This was not only meant to keep the peace of citizens in the nation, it is also meant to restore relationships and hold accountable those who dissuade from it.

through it all. It is that which is precisely the context of "where two or three are gathered in my name, there am I among them."

In verse 16 of the passage above, "if he does not listen" means that after some one-on-one get-together, there might be the need for some intermediaries to help with the reconciliation. Presuming the sin and conflict is between you and someone else, adding an additional mediator or two means that there will now be two or three (or just a shade more) who are all present, pleading and calling for humble repentance of sin and restoration of relationship (remember, the goal is that "you have gained your brother"). This kind of mediation has historical precedent from Deut 19, as mentioned in the footnote above. The now twice-repeated and known phrase of "two or three" (once here in Matt 19, and once prior in Deut 19) along with the phrase "one or two" as well, establishes the reiterative numerical context of what will be coming next in verses 19–20: "Again I say to you, *if two of you agree on earth* about anything they ask, it will be done for them by my Father in heaven. *For where two or three are gathered in my name*, there am I among them."

Jesus loves prayer. Talking to God and listening if perchance he might respond (through guidance in reading his Word), is an incredibly valuable spiritual discipline and a component to a healthy relationship with God and abundant life with him. When we pray, God hears us, and he is always near enough to respond and save us in his desires and plan. However here, in Matt 19, Jesus is not just blandly talking about God's presence in prayer; Jesus is talking about his own presence *in our attempts at reconciling relationships with others.* Jesus mentions his presence when "two or three are gathered in my name" (which, in the direct context refers to the *reason* for their gathering, which is to restore brotherhood and sisterhood that has been severed as a result of sin). It should also be understood that if Jesus is present in the more intense mediation involving "two or three [who] are gathered" then he is also present in the more personal and private one-on-one interaction as well. The context of Matt 19 shows us that no matter how challenging or broad in scope reconciliation needs to be, Jesus is present and with us in it. How encouraging that is, when embraced with fullness and clarity! Let us all understand and be governed by this before giving in to the temptation of apathy and fear.

There was once a story told of an honest ocean captain, in the days of ancient maritime armadas and fleets. One day, the crew called out on the deck of the vessel, "Captain, one enemy ship on the horizon!" The captain, with his thick Spanish accent, declared, "Brrrring me my rrrrred shirt!" The crewmen were confused, but yet obeyed, and the captain donned the red shirt during the fray. All that day when the battle ensued, not a single soul was lost. The entire crew was victorious. Later that night, under calm of the ocean, one seaman asked the captain, "Sir, why did you ask to be brought your red shirt?" The captain explained, his accent as deep as the sea, "While wearing 'ze rrrrred shirt, if I was to become shot, 'zen 'ze crew would not see 'ze blood, and would not become disheartened and give up 'ze fight." The crew member was in awe of the bravery of the captain, and the wisdom of the answer. The very next day, another familiar call came from the watchman on the mast, only this time, much more intense: "Captain, *ten* enemy ships on the horizon!" The captain once again replied, but with a slightly different request: "Brrrring me my brown pants!"

Reconciling relationships is courageously-risky business. It stirs our soul, raises our blood pressure, and just might cause some people to have to figuratively change their pants. But the rewards of working through conflicts and finding health *far outweigh* the deathly scars that remain when apathy and fear take the lead in our lives. And in all things, our courage is not to be seen as impotent and empty. Jesus guides us, calling for right relationships among us, and he is present with us in every step along the way, no matter what is on the horizon.

Yet another objection, or more specifically a situation or question, is as follows: "What if we try to love, and forgive, and reconcile a relationship with another, but the other person is still unwilling to do so themselves?" In the realm of relational reconciliation, this question and scenario are especially commonplace, and a very good inquiry. In seeking to find an answer, it would be valuable for us to understand exactly who Scripture verses—such as those in Luke 6—are written to. Aside from the obvious "everyone"-audience—as indeed the Bible is written to the entire world—specifically, the native audience of Jesus' hearers in Luke 6 were his own immediate followers. Presuming that Jesus' disciples didn't have current conflicts in their midst at that very moment, Jesus was initially speaking to one-half of a relationship pair.

For us today, it would be the same as for you reading this book: imagine, if you will, that someone has some gripe against you, or you have a gripe against someone else. (For many of you reading, this is not difficult to imagine; it is an obvious reality! There may be peoples' faces and names against whom you have conflict, flooding to the foreground of your mind at this very moment.) After you have imagined a challenging relationship, I will now—as the author—presume that you are *not* reading this book *together* in the presence of the person with whom you are fighting. Most reading is done individually, and in isolation. Therein lies the same idea as Jesus' words in Luke 6—where this book, and the biblical truths restated, are being read by one person in a relationship of two.

So with regard to Jesus' words, or this book that is written with the intent of reiterating Jesus' commands, there is only one-half of the broken relationship before the words of Jesus, and his call to love and forgive and make peace and seek reconciliation. That one-half of the friendship is you. Although you can't control others in how they act, and what they think, and what they say, and what they are like, and what they read, you can control *you*. Said in another way, "We are not responsible for people's actions, but we *are* accountable for our reactions."[7]

Simply from the context of Jesus' words in Luke 6, with regards to the question or objection or situation about only one person desiring to make a relationship right, you are always called to make sure that you are that person. Ensure that your heart—which beats for exactly half of the relationship—is ready for reconciliation. This is also, I believe, why it says these words in Rom 12:18 (as shared earlier in this book),

"If possible, so far as it depends on you, live peaceably with all."

In other words, "As much as you can do, make sure that you live at peace with all people." Keep loving them; keep forgiving them; keep praying for them; if you constantly see them, keep smiling before them and greeting them and being kind to them. Ask for God's help to change your vision and how you see them, understanding that the ones who hurt you are the very same ones who are truly hurting inside themselves. Keep looking to have mercy on them. There are some people who might never be intentional about making up with you, because there are some people where it will only take a miraculous act of God to break through their hearts and lead them to be at peace with you. But our initiative and our call is to ensure that whenever, if ever, there is opportunity for reconciliation, we are already peaceable and forgiving and loving toward others, even if they are not receptive at the start.

President Thomas Jefferson, in his active escapades during the formative years of the nation, was once riding on horseback across the country when he and his companions approached a swelled river. A local passer-by was unable to cross on his own accord, so he sought the help of one of the horse riders traversing the same river. He didn't seek the assistance of just anyone, however, but waited to climb aboard the steed of President Jefferson himself, who helped the man to the other side. The others present with the man asked him afterward, "Why did you wait to seek the help of the President over all others?" The man replied, "The President? I didn't know he was the President at all. I just noticed the faces of the riders as they crossed, and

7. Begg, "No Retaliation!"

some of them had a 'No' on their face, while some of them had a 'Yes.' His was a 'Yes' face."[8]

We all would be bettered and blessed to have a "yes" face for reconciliation, regardless of the torrent of the waters to cross in order to attain to it. In other words, let us all be ready to restore a relationship, whether or not the other person is receptive in reply.

The following is a story in my own life that is a testimony to this, as well as a forever-hopeful reminder that God can move in peoples' hearts even if there is brokenness in relationships: I had gotten along very well with a friend and former neighbor. She and I had a great relationship. However, one day I got a phone call from her, where she reamed me out for something that I had done. After unleashing her tirade and getting her pound of flesh, she hung up the phone. It did not take a scholar to discern that this person was angry at me! She felt that I had wronged her significantly. She saw that there was some action that I should have performed, or an inappropriate task that I took part in, that was too much for her to handle. It led to an overflow, and I got an earful of it.

I was completely caught off-guard. To this day I do not even remember what it was that I did, or did not do, that set her over the edge. The important thing is that whether it was memorable, warranted, or otherwise, according to my neighbor and friend I was the culprit. I had offended her. (That is another reason why I feel credible to write such a book and become such a cheerleader for obeying God's Word about relational reconciliation, by the way: not because I am perfect and have perfectly kept it, but precisely because I have failed significantly and have had to work diligently at restoring relationships that I have damaged—whether intentionally or not.) Because I felt so badly over my neighbor's distress, and because God was growing me to become a forever-forgiver and reconciler, I immediately tried calling her back to work through the issue—to no avail. She wouldn't pick up the phone. I only got her voicemail, so I left a very apologetic message for her, telling my neighbor that I was truly sorry for offending her and not doing that thing that she felt I should have done. I shared that I desired to reconcile our relationship and make it new again.

This neighbor and I did not cross paths over the span of probably a few weeks. When I tried to continue to reach out to her, I got nowhere. I couldn't get her on the phone, and our alternating schedules meant that I had not yet seen her in person since the conflict. I was genuinely trying to reconcile our relationship, but it appeared that there was no similar desire in return.

---

8. Menninger, Mayman, and Pruyser, *The Vital Balance*, 22.

Then, one day, I happened to be coming home at the same time as this neighbor and friend. We both saw each other in the driveway, and I walked up to her and began asking for forgiveness again, this time in person. Quite surprisingly, yet divinely-initiated at the same time, she came over and began by apologizing herself as well. She shared that she was sorry for being rude and distant and mean. Even though I was the one who had committed the wrong, my neighbor was the one who was resistant to reconciling, and she felt convicted and ashamed for it. This formerly severed friendship became a simultaneous chorus of confessing our own wrongs, and forgiving each other mutually.

I was so quick to forgive, and so humbled and grateful to have the relationship restored, that my neighbor and friend became blown away and overwhelmed by my gracious gesture. She responded by asking how I could so immediately and easily forgive her and receive her back with joy. She truly could not understand. It was likely that my neighbor had lived with many hurts from many others in the past who were not willing to forgive or embrace relational reconciliation before. She was grappling to try to comprehend.

There is no objection too great, there is no situation too grave, and there is no question too big that Jesus' plan for our hearts and our relationships can't overcome.

∫

I was able to respond by saying that I know how to forgive because God has forgiven me. There were many things in my life that I had done in the past, but because Jesus died on the cross for my sins and I trusted in his grace, God had forgiven me for those very things. I had been ready for the moment of reconciliation and peace with my neighbor and friend, and it became instead something so much greater: a moment of clear explanation of the gospel—the good news that we can be restored to God through Jesus Christ, and be forgiven even though we were undeserving. Through forgiveness of others and the obedience to Jesus' words in Luke 6 and elsewhere, God opened a door to make real and personal how a relationship with Jesus relates to our relationships with others: that on our own we have a broken relationship with God, yet Jesus provided reconciliation between us and him through the cross, and we can show the grace of the cross likewise by extending unconditional love and forgiveness with others.

There is no objection too great, there is no situation too grave, and there is no question too big that Jesus' plan for our hearts and our relationships can't overcome.

Chapter 6

—— ∫ ——

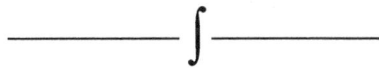

A Healthy Foundation

DWELLINGS ARE AWESOME. NOT only are they fairly essential for comfortable living—as we are helped in our habitation by having some sort of roof over our heads—but they also make for great entertainment. I grew up in the outskirts of the twin cities of Minneapolis and St. Paul, MN; I studied for my undergraduate university degree in the small urban setting of State College, PA; I lived and worked in the city of Williamsport, PA (known by some as "Little Philly"); my family and I lived near, and I received my seminary master's degree, in the large city of Boston, MA; I now am a pastor just around the corner from Buffalo, NY. Call me a city slicker if you will. For me, it is indeed marvelous watching the beautiful sunset over the rolling hills of a rural landscape, but I find it just as magnificent looking dozens of stories up at a high-rise apartment complex or squinting at the sun's reflection off of a glass-plated office city skyscraper. The same God had his hand uniquely in the creation and empowered construction of both.

The diversity of the different kinds of buildings in which we live—whether it be a single-family house, an apartment, a townhouse, a duplex, a hut, a mansion, a tent, or a castle—is additionally fascinating to me. The variety of dwellings not only has captivated the mind of this simple-brained preacher and author, but also the innovative entertainment industry. There are entire television networks based strictly on the production of shows regarding the home. The real estate industry is precisely that—an organized financial framework sustained by where people could and do live. Truth be told, comprehensive global economies have either stood firmly, or been shaken, based on the fallout from financial decisions predicated on or around a person's house (real estate loans, foreclosures, banking institutions, even credit default swaps and investment derivatives). Home certainly is not only where the heart is, but it is also where the wallet is—and where wisdom ought to be as well!

Go figure, then, that approximately 2000 years ago, Jesus used a significant illustration involving the home. In our time looking at healthy relationships and how to avoid relations*lips*, we have centered much of our ground on pragmatic and theologically relational verses in Luke 6 of the Bible. At the very end of this chapter is where Jesus' house analogy arrives, and at the onset it might seem unrelated. However, looked at more closely, it actually provides for us the gravity—no pun intended (as you will see in a moment!)—for this discussion on the importance of having and maintaining healthy relationships. The illustration from Jesus, in Luke 6:46–49, is as follows:

> "Why do you call me 'Lord, Lord,' and not do what I tell you? Everyone who comes to me and hears my words and does them, I will show you what he is like: he is like a man building a house, who dug deep and laid the foundation on the rock. And when a flood arose, the stream broke against that house and could not shake it, because it had been well built. But the one who hears and does not do them is like a man who built a house on the ground without a foundation. When the stream broke against it, immediately it fell, and the ruin of that house was great."

Television shows like "House Hunters" and "Fixer-Upper" and others in the entertainment industry captivate the interest and attention of any of us who like treasure. Within any house, and at any address, is the possibility of an undiscovered gem just waiting to be restored. These T.V. programs have creative entrepreneurs and construction crews renovating old and crusty dwellings in order to make them sparkling and innovative, with the intention of gaining a profit upon resale. But one thing I have yet to see on shows like this is when the repairs needed are beyond the veneer, when the home contracting is structural and foundational.

If a house, apartment complex, or any other building has a faulty foundation, then no amount of fixing-up-ing will be beneficial for the structure. It could have gorgeous adornments within it and the most immaculate four walls known to man, but if that which it is standing upon is shaky then the entire home is in peril. The reality is that the house should have never been built in the first place, and the home is therefore better off being demolished or abandoned than being lived in another second.

Because foundations today are often artificially produced (such as from poured concrete), we think of Jesus' illustration as a bit inconceivable. Who, after all, would build a house on a shaky foundation in the first place? This seems to be the most idiotic idea in the history of real estate![1] In order to bring a more understandable parallel today, I might liken it to building a house in a place where there is *known* impending peril: such as a home intentionally constructed in a flood plain.

A few years after becoming pastor of the congregation where I serve in the Buffalo, NY area, a terrible flood occurred from the creek bed just around the corner from the church building. There was a significant mid-winter cold spell that froze many area waterways, which was followed by a spike of warmer temperatures and rain that led to the over-inundation of these streams and creeks. Once the frozen ice in those creeks cracked and broke apart, it led to giant ice dams that caused tragic spillover of the water into residential neighborhoods nearby the church. Although nobody was seriously hurt, upwards of seventy separate homes in a housing subdivision experienced anywhere from a few inches of water in their basements, to flooding so extensive that it surpassed basement levels and flowed into the first floor of their homes. Coupled with this occurring in the wintertime—and the damage done to home heating furnaces and gas lines—this entire neighborhood was devastated like it had never been seen before.

The church felt incredibly humbled to be present for the community during this time, and to be able to play a part in the disaster relief efforts for these friends and neighbors and community members. Other residents, the town, and community organizations likewise came to everyone's aid. During the recovery, and after looking more extensively at the geography of the region, it became a reminder that one of the reasons there was such devastation is that almost all of the affected homes were originally built in a flood plain. A housing developer, many years' prior, supposed that if a natural waterway was bypassed and dry ground was re-laid, then homes could be built atop that re-routed creek area and financial profit could be

---

1. Aside from Jesus' illustration being difficult to understand in our "mass-produced home" lifestyle and technology today, the visceral reaction to such a foolish venture—to purposefully and intentionally build on a non-solid foundation—may be exactly the kind of reaction that Jesus was anticipating. Not adhering to Jesus' words—with regards to healthy relationships, or any other issue for that matter—can lead *us* to become the buffoon.

made. It seemed like a novel idea at the time, but became a peril during flooding events such as this.

That Sir Isaac Newton certainly was on to something when he was able to articulate the discovery of gravity. With regards to water, regardless of how we redirect or cover up its former path with man-made means, when it spills over its domain it tends to go where it formerly has gone. These "flood plains" are locations just like that: where water has been, or is likely to go, due to lower elevation and the prevalence of flowing water around it. At the date of this book's publishing, there are many state and federal mandates prohibiting new home construction in flood plains. What that local area housing developer had done in the past is now unlawful to do again—and rightly so! With regards to the flooded subdivision nearby the church, however, there did not seem to be restrictions in place at the time.

If the developer could flash forward and predict—or even presume, with conventional and geological wisdom—that there might be a devastating water-saturation event that could destroy these homes and families and contents, then the developer may not have chosen to build in that location. That would have been wise. If there would have been certain knowledge of flooding peril, then it would have been remarkably foolish to continue with construction. This might be a close parallel today to Jesus' illustration in Luke 6:46–49.

In the ancient Near East, before the advent of poured concrete foundations, builders likewise looked—or ought to have looked—for homes with stable footing to build upon. Natural rock, proven hardened soil, brick home mounts, and other similar stability was sought before proceeding on the construction of the house. Anything else would have been seen as utter foolishness. In addition, it was customary in ancient times for many families to share the same dwelling places: the family's founders would have begun construction with a central communal room (like a living room or dining room), complete with kitchen hearth and a few bedroom-type sleeping spaces. As the family grew, other family members would have been given opportunity to build their own private bedrooms circularly off the pre-existing formative rooms of the home. With more and more extended family members living in the same structure as their originating parents, it would not have been uncommon in Jesus' day for many generations to dwell all upon one central foundation.

Imagine the devastation if that foundation was found to be faulty, and the fatalities if the foolish foundation were to erode or be washed away. This is the kind of picture of Jesus' story in these verses. "When the stream broke against [the house without a firm foundation], immediately it fell, and the ruin of that house was great" (Luke 6:49b). The idea is not that the carpet got muddy because water came through the foundation-less floor. Far more perilously, Jesus leads his readers to imagine that regarding the sandy-bottomed home, " . . . immediately it *fell* . . . " Not only would the *home* be in disrepair, but the members of the *family themselves* could potentially be lost. In Jesus' own words applied today, the home and family would be ravaged.

Without any form of linguistic or theological gymnastics, Jesus' analogy strikes similarly true to families of people who fail to heed Jesus' own words regarding how to live healthy and loving and forgiving relationships with others. I have counseled numerous family members whose entire families are ruined, strictly because of unforgiveness and lack of loving merciful compassion the way that God shows and calls for from Luke 6 and elsewhere. The idea of families being in disarray because of not having stable relational foundations couldn't be a better analogy. However, I am not only drawing this illustration out of a vacuum.

Jesus brings this picture—of a house with firm vs. foolish foundations—not just as a relatable analogy, but also most contextually near to his words of relational reconciliation in Luke 6. In the same larger context where Jesus says "forgive" and "give" and "love" and "be merciful" Jesus also describes exactly what it will be like for those who do these things, versus those who do not. "Everyone who comes to me and hears my words and does them, I will show you what he is like" (Luke 6:47). Go figure, Jesus uses a spot-on mental picture of this as a strong house on a proper foundation. Oppositely, "the one who hears and does not do them" (Luke 6:49a) will have relationships come crashing down and be ruined. The stability and health of ourselves—indeed our entire families—is at stake.

When my son was younger, he hurt his thumb inside the house one afternoon while at play. As he screamed in pain, the decibel level from his little throat made it seem as if he had not just hurt his thumb, but that he *severed* his thumb in the playroom. My wife and I rushed into the room to comfort him and see what the matter was. We could hear that he was hurt based upon his cries and his voice (which for us was amazing—that we had any hearing left *period*—because of how loud his screams were). We could sense that he was in pain based on his non-verbal expressions and the agony on his face. But there weren't any other observable signs that he was injured. We examined his thumb, looking for bruising, immobility, blood . . . nothing. He could move his thumb, he could accept pressure on his thumb, all with no recognizable change to his sorrow. There was absolutely no scientific indication of an injury that we could determine, except that our son was squealing in pain. He said that he accidentally hit it on the hardwood floor, or the door, or something in the room, but there was no physical indication of anything of the sort. It was very strange.

We weighed whether we should go to the Emergency Room, or schedule an immediate appointment with his doctor. We decided that we would wait and see what transpired in the moments that followed, and instead gave him an ice pack and an endless supply of hugs. In a short time he calmed down, and eventually went back to playing in the same room. "No doctor visit needed" was our assessment, so we stayed home.

Throughout the next couple of days, our son showed hardly any signs of his "imaginary gruesome" injury. The only exception was on random occasions, when he would say "ouch" only for a moment, then carry on with whatever he was doing before. My wife and I still kept an eye on him and his thumb, and besides a little bit of swelling and residual redness, it still seemed to be fine.

As the swelling and redness continued for a number of days without decline, we eventually decided that we should go into the doctor and get our son's thumb examined. We weren't sure if there was a small fracture at the knuckle, or some kind of internal bleeding that went unrelieved. After being examined, the diagnosis from the pediatrician was an odd internal infection developing inside his thumb. He was given an antibiotic and we were told to soak his thumb in warm water for fifteen minutes a few times each day. When we did, what we discovered was amazing.

The antibiotic helped to eliminate the infection in his thumb. The warm water aided in the extraction of some newly-discovered infected pussy liquid from the site of the injury. All the while, our son's thumbnail continued to grow and essentially separate itself from his thumb at the site of the infection. It might sound a lot worse and more grotesque than it actually was, but for my wife and I—and for our son as well—it was quite an ordeal and a relief at the same time. At last it was an objective confirmation of *something* that had a whole lot of observable *nothing* at first.

After our son's thumb began to look better and the antibiotic and water-soak treatment worked its course, my wife and I started wondering if he would always have a gangly thumbnail at that appendage on his hand (since his nail was in various stages of discoloration due to the mysterious swelling, infection, and water-logged treatment by the doctor). We started to additionally cut away his dead thumbnail with fingernail clippers little by little, as it became bearable by my son for us to do so. One morning after cutting more of his thumbnail, our son rubbed his hand on the carpeted floor of a different room and let out another momentary "ouch!" as he had before. As this kind of painful yawp hadn't occurred in quite a while, I took a closer look at his thumb—which until this moment had been healing quite nicely, still without any knowledge of what it was in recovery from. After an entire duration of time without any resolution, were we still no closer to the quandary behind our son's thumb injury? Or was this recent squeal an indication that there was a breakthrough on the horizon?

> If we willingly choose to hold on to unforgiveness and avoid showing and sharing unconditional love, it will be as if we allow for that splinter of hurt to remain embedded deeply within our hearts.

As I looked more closely at his thumb after the stint of carpet-rubbed play, I saw something: it looked like a small brown speck underneath the edge of my son's thumbnail. After procuring a pair of tweezers, I gingerly pulled out of his thumb not a small speck but a sliver; wait, not a sliver but a *beam*; it was the longest wood-grain splinter I have ever seen. This entire time the cause of the initial pain, the lingering hurt, the occasional "ouch," the continued redness and swelling, the prolonged localized infection, the deadened thumbnail, and the build-up of mucousy puss was all as a result of an *incredibly* long and yet remarkably thin shard of wood lodged and hidden in the flesh underneath my son's fingernail, from a timber of the hardwood flooring in the toy room where my son was playing those days before.

I'm not sure who was more relieved getting the splinter out of his thumb: my son, or myself. The mystery was solved! The comfort was incredible. The healing was complete, and the danger of further damage was eliminated. Who would have thought that a long and tiny speck of wood, hidden from the naked eye and embedded deep within the sensitive tissue underneath the thumbnail, could cause such an ordeal. Especially after its extraction, I felt as if a burden larger than the splinter—more like the size of an Ozark oak—was removed from both my son's life and mine.

The same kind of thing is true in the context of our hearts regarding our relationships with others. It doesn't take very long in our lives together for us to get hurt. Sometimes we are even stabbed very deeply, and often times it can be from those with whom we are at play. Some of the prickliest wounds lie undiscovered by others, embedded deep within the skin and under the hard nail of life. Upon injury, we might find it incredibly difficult to forgive, show love, and seek to reconcile a broken relationship. Especially if the other person is unwilling to reciprocate, our own emotions can begin to swell as we share and show our pain.

Though we might not be able to avoid all hurts in our interactions with others,[2] if we are not careful about it, our own unforgiveness can be like that long splinter underneath the nail of the thumb. If we willingly choose to hold on to unforgiveness and avoid showing and sharing unconditional love, it will be as if we allow for that splinter of hurt to remain embedded deeply within our hearts. Over time it will likely lead to greater anger and harsher emotions, especially revolving around the subject of the one through whom we were hurt. We might have a range of feelings and expressions toward that person, or about that person to others. Unless we move to forgive and have a perspective of unconditional love, we will over time develop a deep relationship infection that will make us sick.

Even with proper pharmaceutical intervention and good-thoughts practices, we will still be simply treating the relationally-infectious symptoms without removing the source. In the same way that my son's swelling and oozing puss secretions lessened because of the antibiotic and water-soak, many people's unhealthy defenses could effectively silence and mask a portion of the illness, injury, or problem. But if the splinter of unforgiveness isn't extracted in our lives, then all it will take is the most innocent of interaction—like a bit of friendly play on the carpet—and the tip of that splinter will get caught on the carpet fiber and stab even more deeply inside of our hearts.

Relief in falling-apart relationships only comes when the splinter is removed. And no, what I mean by that is not that you are justified to "get that prickly person out of here" (anecdotally referring to another individual in this case, of course, even if it is a humorously apropos saying, given the analogy above!). The splinter in our lives is not the other person causing us grief, it is the *grief* that we are holding on to, by choosing not to forgive the other person. Even though forgiving others is hard—just like I get much resistance from my kids when I am now quick on the draw to extract splinters that they get embedded in their hands and feet in the midst of their energetic play—it is, in the long run, one of the most freeing and relief-bringing relational

2. This presumes, of course, that we are not *seeking* to intentionally be the ones who hurt people ourselves. Sometimes those around us are hurt by the unfortunate choices of others—such as an extended family member who carries wounds inflicted by someone in the immediate family, or bitterness and unforgiveness carried around by someone within the context of a friendship community or the local church. Part of the effects of living in a sinful world is that we might offend or hurt others unintentionally. That is why it is so powerfully important to confess sins to one another when we have wronged each other, and forgive others regardless of whether they have confessed their sins to you. Carrying unforgiveness—whether the pain in relationships is malicious or accidental—is a prickly poison that will keep us relationally sick.

exercises that we can practice. Forgiving wrongs, forgetting sins, living at peace, showing unconditional love, and understanding that God lavishes the same upon us through Jesus Christ—these are the things that can make our own lives and relationships healthy even when we are hurt by others.

Whether or not you are convinced by God's Word about relationships, and regardless if you are awed by God's own forgiveness and unconditional love, embracing forgiveness and peace with others is simply a more fulfilling and joy-bringing practice. It is bad enough to experience natural relational trauma in life, like my poor son who gashed his thumb on the gritty hardwood playroom floor. The pain and the damage of life together is inevitable, and is often dulled after the first few passing moments. But not forgiving the person who inflicted the pain, and keeping love from the one who most desperately needs it, is like willingly leaving the splinter in your own finger. It is better to be freed from injury and infection, not to hold on to it as a residual reminder of the initial pain.

In fact, since the choice to forgive and live at peace belongs to you, deciding to forgo it would be equivalent to a malicious dad who leaves the splinter in his son's thumb as a constant reminder of how stupid it was to hurt his hand in the first place. We would be rightly incensed if this was how a parent treated their child who experienced accidental and unintentional injury in the course of their day. Yet why are we tolerant of the same thing in our own lives, and think that it is somehow socially or emotionally acceptable in our case? The true insensitivity—and the empathetic irony—is that by holding on to unforgiveness we take the person who hurt us once (or twice, or a hundred times, all leaving painful slivers inside of us) and we let them hurt us again and again as long as we choose to allow the unforgiveness-splinters to dwell inside.

The splinter is in view; the tweezers are in hand. Will you let go of what others did to you that was wrong, and embrace forgiveness, which is available to you, which is right? Health, stability, relief, and joy await!

Chapter 7

—————∫—————

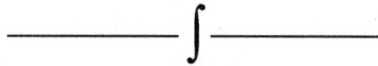

The Best Example of All

AT THE BASE OF every human heart is the need—and the ability—to love. Whether or not you consider yourself a loving person, or whether you are *good* at loving others or loving things, love is somewhere in there. It is a tenant of life, especially life lived together. Even a particular British rock band of yester-yore quipped supposing that love is all that we truly need.

At the core of faith and God's character is the very same thing: *love*. In the Bible's book of 1 John, it says that which is true and what is so fundamental within the Christian faith: as 1 John 4:8 says plainly, "God is love."

If all of this is true, then why do we so often seem to have a hard time in loving others?

Some of you might humbly agree, after reading this book thus far, and admit, "Yep, that's me some/most/all of the time. I find that loving others is hard. Guilty as charged." Others who are much more reserved (and much more dishonest with themselves as well, I believe!) might think, "Oh, no, not I! Well of *course* I love everyone!" But I bet that:

> ▸ If you were put in the *wrong kind of traffic jam*, you wouldn't express actions or attitudes that are very loving.

➤ Or if you were forced to sit right next to that *one person* who you *just can't stand,* then you wouldn't exactly look like or act like a person who is loving.

➤ If someone might look at you the wrong way, or give you the wrong food order at a restaurant; if they have the wrong attitude with you, or if they hold to and believe in the wrong kind of political position . . . then what so easily comes out of you might *not exactly be* the outcome that would warrant the descriptor "love."

Stated again not only out of repetition but also out of importance: if love is such a fundamental need, and if it is so fundamentally a part of the Christian faith, then why do people—and so often, why do so-called "Christians"—seem to have a hard time showing love?

I think that one reason might be because people—whether they are wrongly called "Christians" or not—do not correctly understand (and probably have not correctly experienced) exactly just how God loves us through Jesus Christ. Jesus is the best example of relational reconciliation, extended forgiveness, and love.

One of Jesus' closest disciples, a man named John, has written numerous accounts detailing and explaining things both generically and more specifically for all to read and see. We can look at these things in many of his divinely inspired writings in the Bible, but for the purpose of the loving example of Jesus we need to look no further than 1 John 2:7–11. It says these words:

"Beloved, I am writing you no new commandment, but an old commandment that you had from the beginning. The old commandment is the word that you have heard. At the same time, it is a new commandment that I am writing to you, which is true in him and in you, because the darkness is passing away and the true light is already shining. Whoever says he is in the light and hates his brother is still in darkness. Whoever loves his brother abides in the light, and in him there is no cause for stumbling. But whoever hates his brother is in the darkness and walks in the darkness, and does not know where he is going, because the darkness has blinded his eyes."

As we dig deeper—and as you can also read and see on your own time in the first chapter of 1 John—there is evident in John's writings quite a bit of repetition.

> ▸ There is almost a constant use of the dichotomy of "light" and "darkness" coming from John's pen.[1]

> ▸ There is this regular theme of, in essence, those who are *truly* followers of Jesus Christ, and those who are "liar[s]" and *not* living in the truth.[2]

> ▸ And there is also a reiteration of the idea of "commandment[s]" right before the verses above, found in 1 John 2:7–11.[3]

In John's writings—indeed in even the most recent sentences and paragraphs above—he wrote that we could know who has known Jesus based upon whether or not they "keep [or obey] his [that is, Jesus'] commandments" (1 John 2:4) and "walk in the light" (1 John 1:7) where "the love of God is [truly] perfected" (1 John 2:5) in them. But now reading 1 John 2:7–11, we see more specificity to all of that, as John brings up this commandment of a person "lov[ing] his brother" like we see in 1 John 2:10:

> "Whoever loves his brother abides in the light, and in him there is no cause for stumbling . . . "

Before going any further, I think it might be valuable to pause and clarify what could be some confusion about the idea of John talking about an "old commandment" and a "new commandment" in his writings. It actually doesn't have to be confusing, because John has written about Jesus' commandments before. We can see that in another one of John's writings in the Bible—John 13:34–35, which I have also referenced earlier in this book[4]—where we read such similar words from John's pen, this time writing direct quotations spoken by Jesus:

> "[Jesus speaking:] A new commandment I give to you, that you love one another: just as I have loved you, you also are to love one another. By this all people will know that you are my disciples, if you have love for one another."

You can see, in reading these words, that this is *not* John's first rodeo with regards to loving others as a commandment of Jesus. In fact, even before Jesus spoke these words, the idea—even the command—to "love others" was not anything new even in the Old Testament. Once again, just as I mentioned earlier in this chapter, love is *such* a foundation not only to our

---

1. See, for example, the usages of "light" and "darkness" in 1 John 1:5, 6, and 7.
2. See 1 John 1:6, 8, 10; also 1 John 2:4 and 5.
3. Namely in 1 John 2:3 and 4.
4. See the responses to "Question 1" and "Question 2" of the Relations*l*ips Quiz earlier.

hearts, our abilities, and our souls, but also to God's own character—which we are *all* to pursue and obey and live for!

But here in John 13:34–35, what makes Jesus' statement and command somehow "new" is that our love is to be extended like it says in the middle of John 13:34, "just as I [Jesus] have loved you." Prior to this statement by Jesus, loving others was predominantly thought by many to be reciprocal, non-sacrificial, and selfish.

▸ "If you slap *my cheek*, then I'll slap *yours*."[5]

▸ "If you take *my cloak*, then I'll take *yours*."[6]

▸ "If you start showing *me mutual love*, then mutual love is what will come to you and *yours*."

But then Jesus showed up. And he talked—and lived—sacrificial and unconditional love. We even see that in John 13 by looking at the surrounding context: here Jesus is with his disciples at the Last Supper when he says these words about love, and Jesus is talking about how he will be *betrayed* by others, and *die on the cross*. It is in the midst of others' hatred toward him and it is in embracing this sacrifice of the cross where Jesus is sharing about how he will give himself to the uttermost. *Right in that very moment* he says, " . . . just as I have loved you, you also are to love one another."

Back to 1 John 2:8 now—which was John's later writing—we see that this love, this "new commandment" that is really an "old commandment" because it originated in God, is like it says in verse 8, a thing "which is true in him." In other words, God's sacrificial and unconditional love is true in Jesus, as seen by his sacrifice on the cross. And the logic follows, as it follows in the words of verse 8, that it also ought to be a thing "which is true [also] in you." Because since Jesus has died and we can see it—since we are on *this side* of the timeline of history and the timeline of the cross—then "the darkness [of this lack of knowledge, at least] is passing away and the true light is already shining." In other words, we are not in the dark anymore about what Jesus meant in John 13. We can *see*—and in fact we *must see* and understand—the love of God in the cross of Jesus Christ, in order to be in the light and in order to truly and fully love one another. The example of love as seen in Jesus really is the best example of all.

---

5. This is part of what made Jesus' teaching in the famed "Sermon on the Mount" in Matt 5–7—and here specifically in Matt 5:38–42, for example—so powerful: even though it seemed to run contrary to what the Old Testament law said, Jesus showed that in actuality *he* (Jesus himself) was giving the law its *fullest* fulfillment (see Matt 5:17).

6. See the footnote immediately above.

All of our lives are best lived in the *light* of the knowledge of Jesus Christ; his death on the cross, his sacrificial and unconditional love for whoever believes in him, and the life and the love that he still gives because he is alive and is interceding for those who desire to live in him by faith. And one reason that many people—even many Christians—do not fully and sacrificially and unconditionally love others is because, quite frankly, we have not yet fully embraced and understood God's love for us through Jesus. If we got that—if we *truly* understood how Jesus loves us—then our ability to love others would be a piece of cake! We would be able to realize that if *we* are shown love like Jesus loves, then we would be hypocritical darkness-dwellers if we were to show anything else than love to everyone else, and specifically to those in the body of Christ, the church.

It's like this: Jesus *died* for you. That is the "as I have loved you" new commandment that we are supposed to love by. So, ponder these stark questions:

> ‣ When was the last time *you died* for someone else?

What's that? Hasn't happened? Clearly, because if it is true that "dead men tell no tales," then it is also true that if you were dead, you wouldn't be able to be reading this one, either!

> ‣ Then when was the last time *you drastically sacrificed something of yours* for someone else?

No recollection? Our lack of regular and realistic sacrifice is the most fundamental indicator that human beings have become selfish creatures. And our humble responses to these questions show that we are missing the momentousness of the example of love as seen in Jesus. What if we drove the questions home with greater specificity:

> ‣ When was the last time you turned off the T.V. for someone else? (Or is the truth of your living room more like this: "Don't bother me, Woman, I'm watchin' the game!")

> ‣ When was the last time you put your smartphone down for someone else? (If this situation hasn't happened to you yet, then let me humbly alert you to the fact that others around you *have noticed* that you selfishly ignore human beings in order to pay attention to a three-inch by six-inch rectangular electronic box! It didn't take long for my two-year old toddler twins to walk up to me in our home as I was replying to someone's text message or trolling the news headlines or viewing the weather forecast or checking the score of the big game, only to hear

one of those cute two-year-olds say, "Daddy, put the phone down! Come and play with me!" Yep . . . I'm busted.)

Here are a few more questions to ponder as to whether we are loving others sacrificially in light of the example of Jesus' love for us:

> When was the last time you *went without food* for someone else?

> When was the last time you *woke up early* or *went without sleep* to be with someone else?

> When was the last time you *left your vacation ahead of time* for someone else?

> When was the last time you *let go of something you liked* or the *schedule you preferred* for someone else?

Not only are these questions humbling to process regarding others around us, but for Christians they might even be more humbling to think about relative to our attitudes, actions, and love for the church—which is likely a fine and accurate application of 1 John 2:9, 10, and 11 when it says that we are to love "[our] brother." Once again, in brief, when was the last time you *truly loved* someone else "just as I [Jesus] have loved you"?

When my wife and I discovered that she was pregnant with twins, her obstetrician began scheduling her for more regular ultrasound appointments. It was determined that there was a possibility that this pregnancy could be considered somewhat higher risk: my wife was a bit older than she had been before, she has a medical blood condition that tends to make her pregnancies more precarious, and bearing multiples in general is typically riskier than a singleton pregnancy. It seemed like a wise medical decision to keep an extra eye on the little ones in utero.

At one of the ultrasound appointments, the sonogram technician was able to see the two tiny tikes in my wife's womb, but was not able to discern if they were each within their own amniotic sacs. If each twin was in their own sac, then healthy development throughout the pregnancy was much more likely; if the two twins shared one sac, without any separating membrane wall, then the chances of one of the twins not fully developing or even passing away before birth was significantly higher. During the ultrasound it was determined as well that our twins were considered "monochorionic" (meaning they both shared one placenta in the womb, as opposed to being separately-developing with two placentas in two locations in the uterus). Putting both of these observations together led to the ultrasound technician and the doctor's determination: this pregnancy was of a *much* higher risk than initially anticipated.

If our twins were indeed found to not only be monochorionic (sharing one placenta), but also monoamniotic (sharing one amniotic sac in the womb), then the possibility of hindered development would have been likely due to one twin's healthy growth *at the expense of the other*. This precarious complication (which was one plausible condition among others) is called "twin-to-twin transfusion syndrome." Essentially, in twins that are both sharing the mother's lone placenta and residing in one amniotic sac, there is an increased risk that the twins would innately sense a kind of developmental disharmony, since one placenta and one sac is the normal uterine environment for only a single-child pregnancy. In many instances of twin-to-twin transfusion syndrome, one twin becomes a sort of "donor," and instinctively begins to cease their own development and forego vitality for the sake of the other developing twin. Imagine a middle school boy and girl, both of whom have a crush on each other, stumbling upon the last plate of food in the school cafeteria's lunch line. One of the lovebirds certainly would forego their portion so that the other could eat and be satisfied. Now imagine that this plate-sharing was required all year, and that the same one of the pair continued to be given the full serving on the plate; after a while, the increasingly hungrier child would be invariably less healthy, where the one given the other's serving would be just as they ought to have been all the while.

This possibility—of my wife's pregnancy becoming this risky, and of our twins' vitality becoming more uncertain—certainly rattled our confidence, and tested our trust and dependence on God for his plan in our lives and with our pre-born children. Additionally, researching this actual occurrence—of a kind of innate, selfless, sacrificial subservience of pre-born babies in the womb—absolutely blew me away. Although some would see the in-utero sacrifices of a twin-to-twin transfusion syndrome being simply a natural outworking of Darwinism and the evolutionary process,[7] I saw it as such an incredibly compelling example of the innate and instinctive

---

7. Darwinism, or the evolutionary process in mind, is the idea of the "survival of the fittest"—namely the notion held by evolutionary scientists that species became extinct over billions of years primarily because they were not as sustainable as those who have evolved into what they are today. If you were to research more deeply the medical outworkings of twin-to-twin transfusion syndrome, I believe you would see something different than "natural selection" at work—for example, the "donor" twin in this scenario doesn't just instantly succumb to non-vitality because it is self-selected as such, but instead it rather brilliantly and innately begins to lessen development of its *non-vital organs* first, thereby continuing its own growth in case of later medical intervention for its own survival, etc. Suffice it to say that this footnote and this book is neither the time nor the place to debate the accuracy of Darwin's worldview. I have great dignity and appreciation for the scientific community; however, I place far more credence in the supremacy of God than over natural selection and evolutionary Darwinism.

sacrifice that is available to anyone at our core. If pre-born babies are able to give up their own nutrients that are needed for their development and survival in order to provide for another, without even having to be told to do so in scoldings or lectures or books about relational reconciliation, then certainly we as people are able to muster up the necessary courage and humility in order to let go of our own selfishness in order to see a wrong relationship be made right.

My wife's twin pregnancies turned out with a wonderfully redemptive ending: it was discovered at a subsequent ultrasound appointment that there *was* an amniotic wall found between the two. So, they each were sustainably surviving in their own amniotic sacs after all (and therefore the danger of nutrient sacrifice and deficiency such as is seen in twin-to-twin transfusion syndrome all but disappeared). Our tiny little "womb-mates" were born vibrantly healthy and without any complications. However, they have now grown into elementary school aged competitors who share toys in one moment and fight brutally for the same toy in the next. We don't even need an ultrasound technician to discern that. Go figure. (Looks like my next writing project will be a pop-up picture book entitled "Relations*lips For Kids!*")

It is evident, in our society today, that there is less and less sacrificial love shown for one another. The reason we all, I believe, find it difficult to show love from time to time is because we don't truly understand how Jesus showed his love for us. If we truly could grasp the cross—the suffering, the agony, the separation from God the Father, the carrying of our sin and bearing God the Father's wrath—if we truly grasped that, then every time we got frustrated with another person (or more especially someone in the church), we would break with guilt and conviction because of our hypocrisy.

> "Oh, how could I *think* this way! How could I *act* this way! How could I *live* this way! How could I *speak* this way! Jesus has shown *nothing but love* for me! And yet here I am, being grumpy and judgmental and self-righteous and bitter and irritated and antagonizing and not loving to someone else?! God doesn't feel *any of that* toward me! How in the world can I justify feeling that way toward anyone else?"

If our understanding of God's compassion through Jesus Christ truly took over in our lives, then our compassion for others would likewise take over and become a new kind of love for others.

Something old and normal somehow becomes something new. And it's love. How amazing! And how needed in our world today.

Chapter 8

—————∫—————

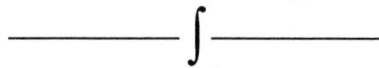

Relations*l*ip Review

A Blessing (Not a Curse)

I HAVE MENTIONED EARLIER in this book that my background, prior to authoring and pastoring, was in teaching. Informing young minds is a wonderful responsibility . . . made significantly simpler with textbooks. For as long as there has been education, there has been the content which frames that education. Since the advent of the printing press, books that enhance learning have been used in classrooms around the globe. Granted, more affluent school systems have arguably greater access to textbooks, furthering the urgency and the need for us to pursue equality in districts and educational systems worldwide. But from colonial one-room schoolhouses to the projector and smartboard-containing high-tech classrooms of today, teachers and students alike are blessed with texts.

This book as a whole is a type of that text. No, this is not a classroom textbook, although the material within certainly would help us proceed through the school of hard knocks! With sincerity, Jesus, "the Word [who] became flesh" (John 1:14), has spoken great truths about healthy relationships with God and with others, and I am simply a herald proclaiming it yet again. Even this chapter within this book is a kind of review of this heralding, but because of the frequency with which we forget Jesus' words I feel that its restatement is important and all the more valued. If something like maintaining healthy relationships is so integral that Jesus shares its truth in repeated commands and reiterated stories and everything between, then we would be wise to hear its truth many times over ourselves. After all, in both teaching and preaching—and also in writing—an important tactic is reiteration. In other words, it is extremely central to repeat one's self. To say it again, repetition is a jewel that helps the mind to remember. That is why redundancy is so valuable. (I hope you have gotten the idea!).

I remember as a student in the classroom, either in speech communication courses or in preparation for preaching, that the target adage should be: "Tell them what you're going to tell them, then tell them, then tell them what you've told them." Intro, body, and conclusion. Content repeated is not at all to be discarded—especially if it is something so valuable as relational reconciliation, where our lives and our friends and our families and even our blood pressure hangs in the balance! This chapter, a review or primer of sorts, is to be a welcomed repetition of the joys and needs of relationship regeneration, and we would indeed be blessed to read and hear and process it again.

I used to work with a gentleman who, when asked, "Hey, how are you?" had an atypical response. His reply was not the normal "I'm fine," or "I'm good," or things like that. He responded, "Man, I'm *blessed*." Maybe some of you reading even respond to others with words or phrases like that. When I heard that response to such a simple and normal social interaction, it made me stop and think, "Now *there's* a guy that's got somethin' goin' right!" The truth is that we all want to be blessed; we all need to be blessed; we all desire to be blessed.

Now, I feel the need to share a caveat at this time, because some might have the daytime talk-show phenomenon in your mind right now—the kind of thing where a T.V. host riles up the crowd's emotions right before giving everyone in the studio audience "a free car!" Truthfully, from this humble author, that ain't happenin' (to say it eloquently!). With the constantly-growing small village of children that reside in my house, my wife and I will be blessed enough not to have to sell our own non-vital organs just to pay for clothes during our kids' growth spurts. I will say, however, that I actually have chosen to show my philanthropy and blessing in some respects through the writing of this book: in fact, 100% of the proceeds of the sale of this book are going directly to the charity "Feed The Children." (Ahem . . . *my* children . . . !)

All humor aside, blessing is spectacular. We often look for financial or material blessing, as if that is what is most primordial and substantive in our lives. However, a far greater blessing than any kind of monetary or material talk show giveaway is the kind of blessing of the heart and soul. In fact, this kind of blessing is all over the Bible, from some of its earliest pages forward.

The ancient Near East—which is the place in the modern-day Middle East and parts of Asia and Africa—is where God's revelation to humankind in Scripture came about in history. We see in Scripture, as well as in other ancient

Near Eastern historical writings, that it was commonplace in the culture for many things to revolve around blessings and curses (or afflictions, to think of it in another term). Ancient rulers prescribed blessings for their servants and subjects who served the kingdom well, and forecasted curses (or, again, afflictions or consequences) if they did not obey. Much of the language of the Old Testament of the Bible, especially God's covenants with his people,[1] regularly used language revolving around "blessings" for obeying, and "curses" for disobeying. The clearest example of this is found in Deut 28, although verbiage the same is seen elsewhere in the earliest pages of the Old Testament.

Even Jesus spoke this kind of way, in his famed "Sermon on the Mount" to his disciples and followers, seen in Matt 5 and following. The central biblical passage regarding relations/ips that has grounded this book, that being Luke 6, is simply a parallel account of Jesus' same sermon in Matt 5. Both places begin Jesus' discourse with blessings, and Luke 6 continues it with a form of curses as well:

> " . . . And he [Jesus] lifted up his eyes on his disciples, and said: 'Blessed are you who are poor, for yours is the kingdom of God. Blessed are you who are hungry now, for you shall be satisfied. Blessed are you who weep now, for you shall laugh. Blessed are you when people hate you and when they exclude you and revile you and spurn your name as evil, on account of the Son of Man! Rejoice in that day, and leap for joy, for behold, your reward is great in heaven; for so their fathers did to the prophets.
> But woe to you who are rich, for you have received your consolation. Woe to you who are full now, for you shall be hungry. Woe to you who laugh now, for you shall mourn and weep. Woe to you, when all people speak well of you, for so their fathers did to the false prophets.'" (Luke 6:20–26)

Maybe coming across in a bit of different form, the similarities between ancient Near Eastern contextual norms of "blessings" and "curses" is still familiar within Jesus' words. This verbiage was significantly common at that time. Jesus shares with the people that they are "blessed" for following God with a certain kind of heart and demeanor; then Jesus conversely shares that they are to be in "woe" for having another kind of life and perspective.

Then, after this "blessed . . . [and] woe . . . " introduction, Jesus continues, and shares these amazing truths that often get overlooked, more often not obeyed, and what lead to the difference between relationships and

---

1. Examples of this are God's promises to Abraham that his descendants would number the stars of the sky and the sand on the seashore, and God's covenant with Moses and the people of Israel regarding their entry into the Promised Land.

relations*l*ips. At this stage of reading this book, we can all be in almost basic agreement with the truth that lives are to be lived with one another. Nobody is meant to be an island. We all interact with others every day. And regardless of whether you are the most recluse person in existence or the world's largest social butterfly, we also have some kind of relationship with God in one way or another.

I mentioned earlier in this writing that you might not have a close relationship with God through Jesus Christ, nor even desire to validate the truths of the Bible. That is still entirely plausible, and does not in the least diminish the real needs that we have to work on restoring broken relationships on earth. Not caring about the history or validity of the United States Constitution still means that you are nonetheless governed by it. Not knowing or honoring basic laws still means that a person is held accountable to adhering to them. Everyone's relationship with God—whether you believe and acknowledge him or not—is still, and more importantly, the greatest relationship needing restoration above all. The point is that even if we all have exemplary relationships with others, we are constantly in need of restoring our relationship with God. And whether you feel near to God or don't even believe in him is no justification to skimp out on reconciliation. Non-believing does not mean non-existing.[2] We must get our relationships right with others and with God as well.

Some people have a personal relationship with God in Jesus Christ, and as a result a close fellowship (or nearness) to God. Others have a personal relationship with Jesus, but feel distant from nearness and intimacy with God. There are even others who still have neither any personal relationship with Jesus, nor any closeness to God at all. Nonetheless, everyone will still have a relational accounting to God one day. The truth is that God created us as people to be in relationship—with God in Jesus Christ, and with others.

It didn't take very long, in the Bible's first pages, for God to create the first person on earth and then right thereafter say, "It is not good that the man should be alone" (in Gen 2:18). We, as a people, are regularly in relationship with God and with others. And exactly how healthy those relationships are will determine whether we are a person who is "blessed" or afflicted ("cursed" or in "woe" in other words).

---

2. The renowned nineteenth century German philosopher and atheist, Friedrich Nietzsche, took his disbelief to the next level when he famously penned "God is dead"; see Nietzsche, *The Gay Science: or The Joyful Wisdom*, 43, 75. Ironically enough, it wasn't God who died, but Nietzsche certainly did, in August, 1900. Even though it is not quoted anywhere, the anecdote "Nietzsche is dead" (says God) would be quite apropos here. Poor Friedrich never got to see his own anti-religious philosophies become satirical punch lines . . . although I do feel the need to give God the last word all the same; see Ps 14:1.

It makes brilliant sense then, that the words that Jesus shares right after his "blessed . . . [and] . . . woe . . . " language in Luke 6 are the core context of this book. The next verses in Luke 6:27–49 are relational words that are so profound and yet also so simple (and often times still so difficult to live and apply). These are words that have so much to do with blessed relationships, in order to avoid the curses of relations*lips*.

The reality is, however, that regarding Jesus' words—indeed, the Bible in general—they appear to be the most infrequent words before our eyes and likely the last words on our minds. Even if we do read heralded reminders of God's Word (like is this book), or if we pour over the biblical text itself, in the heat of relational frustration it is seen that our reading of the Bible was really a *glossing-over* of eternal truth. Instead, we so quickly get ticked off over what that person just put on Facebook, or we get miffed beyond belief about that one-finger gesture given by another driver on the road. We as people become intensely and immediately frustrated about what so-and-so just said or did, that it shows that Jesus' words never really stayed rooted very deeply; they instead seem to have disappeared precisely when we have needed them the most.

Jesus spoke words like "love your enemies, do good to those who hate you, *bless* those who *curse*[3] you, pray for those who abuse you" (Luke 6:27–28, emphasis mine). He shared, "as you wish that others would do to you, do so to them" (verse 31), "be merciful" (verse 36), and "judge not . . . condemn not . . . forgive" (verse 37). These are incredibly integral relational words to read and be reminded of and applied.

In addition, Jesus shared the same kinds of things in *metaphors* and *stories* and *examples* of illustration also in Luke 6:

> ⟩ Want to be *blind*, or the one who can *see*? (verses 39, 42–43)

> ⟩ Want to be a faithful *disciple*? (verse 40)

> ⟩ Want to be a *good* fruit-bearing tree, or a *bad and dead* tree? (verses 43–44)

> ⟩ Want to be a *good person*, or *evil*? (verse 45)

> ⟩ Want to be *disobedient*, or *obey Jesus*? (verse 46)

> ⟩ Want to be a weak, foolishly built, crumbling house on a *shaky foundation*, or a rock-solid house that will *stand*? (verses 47–49)

---

3. Potentially another instance of the common cultural verbiage of "blessing" and "curses," or at least a revisiting of Jesus' mention of the "blessed . . . [and] woe . . . " language earlier in Luke 6.

Probably the most amazing of all of God's words to us regarding biblical reconciliation is that Jesus, when speaking to his followers, reminds us that not even God is hypocritical . . . because God does these "blessing" things himself, graciously abounding his love and forgiveness and faithful mercy and goodness upon us. Let us be reminded that:

> God loves you, even though you and I are sinful before him. (Rom 5:8)

> God is kind to you, even though you and I are not thankful—and when we instead often act quite evil. (Luke 6:35)

> God is merciful to you, even though you and I are often unmerciful to others. (Luke 6:36)

We might hear encouragements like those above every once in a while; maybe listen to sermons like this preached in churches here or there; we might even read this from time to time in the Bible or Christian devotionals. But we are still faced daily with difficult people and difficult relationships. Truth be told, for some of you reading this, it might be difficult to accept that the common denominator in all of your disjointed and dysfunctional relationships is *you*. It may be a struggle to accept, but it is at least entirely possible that *you* are the cause of *your own* relational conflicts, and until you reconcile your bitterness before God and others then nothing at all is going to change. Before God, and in relationships with others, we carry our sin and shortcomings like gross baggage; in the words of Isa 59:12,

" . . . For our transgressions are multiplied before you, and our sins testify against us; *for our transgressions are with us*, and we know our iniquities . . . " (emphasis mine).

Or said another way, from the words of an ancient Greek scholar: "The problem with that man is that he takes himself with him wherever he goes."[4]

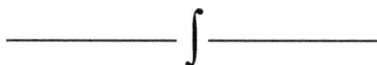

"The problem with that man is that he takes himself with him wherever he goes."

---

4. This is attributed to Socrates, although no direct citation is known.

I can humbly and humiliatingly absolutely relate. I am not at all perfect in this regard. I have made many mistakes in friendships, in family dynamics, in church family relationships, and in my relationship with God. But thanks be to God that he has been doing a work in me over the years, and praise him that his Word is tried and true and always able to be followed in second chances, and third chances, and fourth chances, and so on.

How we treat others . . . if gruff and rough and not like Christ, then it certainly will lead to some relations*l*ips and many "woes." But on the other hand, if we treat others with the mercy and compassion and grace and forgiveness and love of God in Jesus Christ, following after him . . . then we will truly be blessed.

Chapter 9

$$\int$$

Relationship Revolution

AT THE START OF this book, you heard me state that we all have the need for a relationship revolution. For far too long, and with far too many casualties in our wake, we have been living with relations*lips*, rather than in healthy relationships. Offending others or feeling offended ourselves, withholding forgiveness or not seeking forgiveness with each other, choosing to bury our feelings rather than investing in the hard work of reconciling the relationships that have slipped from good health, we all are far too often choosing the weak and carnage laden path. We need a revolution.

The word "revolution" might conjure up different images to different people. For many, we might think of the "American Revolution," that violent stand of independence that the forefathers of the United States took against the oppression and tyranny of the British Empire during the days of early North American colonization. It might seem to carry pictures of muskets and bayonets, of bloody flesh wounds and black powder smoke pouring over a misty battlefield. A simple visit to the monuments of New England, or the hollowed grounds of Gettysburg instantly bring back imagery associated with this word.

But also, at the heart of the word "revolution" is the lingual root "revolve." Mathematically (sorry, folks, for another numerical and geometric analogy!), a revolution is a *turning*—a kind of rotational shift—of an object in order for there to be a placement of a new image. A shape that has a revolution around a certain loci is that same shape, only turned to be in a new orientation. This root-word picture might be more savvy and nuanced, but it is nonetheless relevant. With regards to a "relationship revolution," I find it helpful to process both word descriptions in order to move forward into what is needed before us.

We have previously spent considerable time in chapter 4 ("Get Ready for Some Changes") describing how God desires for us all to *change* in order to maintain healthy relationships. In this respect, the call again to change is helpful for us to view our need for a revolution of relational proportions. Many times, we are pragmatically required to *revolve* our preferences, expectations, pride, vision, schedule, and so on, in order to work more intentionally on having and maintaining healthy relationships. I cannot tell you how many times I have begun a week, with my calendar/planner busy and fully scheduled, only to have to *revolve* it entirely in order to reconcile with a friend because there were hurts in a relationship that were brought to my attention at the end of the week before. Or, when navigating my own thoughts for my own plans, I have seen the need to revolutionize my day in order to rotate around the relational needs of others for the cause of good interpersonal health. So, there is a sense that a "relationship revolution" is a turning or rotating or *revolving* around a new priority—namely, restoring a broken friendship—because God calls for its priority over many other things.

There is also the value of seeing a relational revolution in strong and militaristic terms . . . however not as your minds might originally think. You see, we are not bettered if we emulate the carnage that others have caused us in relationship. We are quite able to turn relationships into relations*lips* fairly easily, and it is not an honorable outcome to say the least! An American Revolutionary War type of mental picture is not the idea of fighting *each other* in relationships. No, the battle-mantra ideal of a revolution is that we must be fighting *the fighting*.

I grew up with formative memory of the conflicts of the first Persian Gulf War. The attention to hostile actions in the Middle East was prevalent in many newspapers, magazines, radio programs, and television broadcasts. The media's fascination with war likely led to its heavy coverage, further because we had not seen as much engagement in active battle in a number of years. As the technology of weaponry had changed, so did the interest of television viewers and reporters alike. Although the United States still engaged in battle array across the desert sand with tanks and tan-camouflaged uniforms, there was an entirely different battle-within-the-battle being waged in the skies.

I am certainly not an expert in that era of Middle Eastern warfare; however my memory (and the frequent media coverage) was drawn to the military tactics of enemies launching missiles into the sky. Iraqi "scud" missiles were flying through the air, with the intention of wreaking havoc on military targets and civilian villages in Kuwait and other parts of the region. Interestingly enough, the U.S. military response was to launch missiles of our own . . . however, not at the enemy's land-based targets (although that has occurred for many years the same). Rather, the United States deployed "Patriot missiles" whose individual missions were to fly through the air and take out the already-airborne missiles of the enemy.

This missile-on-missile warfare seemed to be a fascinating new development in armed conflict at the time. Although it likely was not new in the history of weaponry, it certainly appeared new to the American people. I still remember the indelible images of news cameras showing a downed scud missile, busted apart and laying on the ground in some remote desert region or in some non-descript part of a village, blown out of the sky by a U.S. Patriot missile. It seemed revolutionary—and, in a military sense, it was a revolution of "fighting fire with fire" (as the saying goes), shooting down missiles with other missiles. Or, in another sense, *fighting the fighting*.

If we adhere to a somewhat similarly vigilant approach, we might just be able to have a valuable "relationship revolution" with the same kind of mental picture. If the attacks of cultural norms and our spiritual adversary, the devil, encourage us to just "let time heal all wounds," or seek reciprocity and be mean to those who are mean to you, then we would be right to launch the counter-cultural missiles of unconditional love and hard-work reconciliation against notions such as these. Again, I am not advocating for us to fight with others who seem to enjoy fighting with us; rather, if we fight against our own instincts to *want to fight back*, then we will essentially be shooting others' missiles out of the sky—or shooting down (or holding back) our own missiles of anger and resentment before they hit the target, thereby opening the door for reconciliation within our hearts. An appropriate revolution would not be *fighting the fighting with fighting*, but rather *fighting the fighting with forgiveness, reconciliation, and unconditional love.*

Whichever is your preferable mental picture associated with the word "revolution," we are still significantly in need of it. Our relationships are in need of it. Our stress levels are in need of it. Our neighborhoods are in need of it. Our families are in need of it. Our workplaces, and healthy production, is dependent upon it. Our churches are called by God to be fertile grounds for it. And all relationships would be bettered because of it.

Let's embrace the revolution.

Relationship Revolution

In obedience to God's Word, and understanding the love, forgiveness, and relationship Jesus Christ desires for me and others, I hereby resolve to the following:

> ➤ I will commit to *loving everyone unconditionally*, for this is the way that God loves me. (Luke 6:27 and 35; John 13:34–35; 1 John 4:7–8)

> ➤ I will commit to *forgiving others first and always*, because God has graciously forgiven me. (Matt 6:14–15 and 18:21–35; Luke 6:37)

> ➤ I will commit to *being peaceful and getting along* with everyone in the church, because God desires for peace to be a fruit of the Holy Spirit inside of me. (Rom 12:18; 2 Cor 13:11; Gal 5:22–23)

> ➤ I will commit to *pursuing right and reconciled relationships* with others, because through Jesus Christ God has pursued a right and reconciled relationship with me. (Matt 5:23–24; 2 Cor 5:17–21)

Appendix I

$$\int$$

The Famously Misnamed Parable

I HAVE SOMEWHAT OF a large family. Four kids walking around in public spaces with one parent—or even two—often times draws stares from passers-by. This is because the internalized comic response of most people regarding progeny is that after one child is borne to a couple, people celebrate; after two children, people feign a smile; after three or more, people begin to think or say, "You know where they come from, don't you?"

Our somewhat large family are friends with other even larger families. Five kids . . . or six . . . or even seven or more . . . yep, a family like that wrangling with everyone at an outing usually requires a travel agent and a personal parental assistant. So, I can appreciate stories involving families—large or small—and how they hit home for all of us.

One story was of a particularly large family, with an absolutely ridiculous number of kids. Children too many to even remember correctly, it seems. To boot, this family decided that camping in the woods by the lake would somehow be a good decision for a family vacation. But to their credit, they pulled it off without a hitch year after year. They rented a cabin with a plethora of bunkbeds, and spent their days relaxing by the dock. Some of the kids swam in the cool water under the hot sun; others caught minnows and built lakeshore sand castles on the beach. The older kids went for hikes; the younger ones searched for wildflowers. At the end of every day, they all gathered together by the fire for an evening meal with the whole troupe. On one of those years, during one of those days at the dinner time rendezvous, everybody came back . . . except for the youngest daughter. She was missing, and no one knew where she was.

The father instantly sank into a state of panic. He had everyone stay put, and ran off to hopefully find his child. He scoured the lakeshore; no signs of his little girl. He called for her in the woods; he received no response. Wondering if his voice was lost amidst the thickest trees, he ran deeper into the wooded boundary until he finally found her, gathering multi-colored berries. "I wanted to make an art project for you, Daddy, and I saw these beautiful berries of many different colors that I thought would make it look so pretty!" He scooped her up in his arms, elated and relieved that she was no longer lost and not the slightest bit hurt. Returning back to the rest of his family, who all worried and prayed and remained by the fire safely so they too would not get lost, they all now enjoyed each other's presence in relief and joy like never before.

The story is incredibly touching on so many levels. It is a bit counter-cultural in terms of logistics, however. A large space, with many perils; a full family, with so many members; if the pawns in the story weren't people but instead were products in an industry, mathematical logistics might have said, "Forget the lost one; focus on the many that you still have and that yet remain." If it was a cache of a hundred one-dollar bills from a garage sale profit, for example, only a fool would leave $99 waiting in the wings in search for a measly buck. I can personally attest to this industry standard, as I once was delivered a brand new electronic tablet by mistake from a tech company. Once I notified them of their error, they determined that rather than tracking down their missing piece of hardware at my doorstep, it was easier and more cost-beneficial for them to simply allow for me to keep it. It appears that searching for a lost item—along with shipping, inventorying, and re-stocking the object that is missing—is not always the most optimal solution.

However, in this story, the daughter was not an object, but rather a precious child. As a result, the dad would have been vilified if, after receiving news from his wife that their youngest daughter was missing, said, "Eh, we've got how many kids, Honey? One less wouldn't hurt us that much. In fact, it might even be better off for our financial picture. Plus, if I go out wandering to find that wayward missing child, then I could get lost myself, or another one of you might leave the campfire and try to find us after so long, and you could get lost too. We should just let her be. She's only the runt of the litter after all. Plus, it serves her right for not coming back like she was supposed to. Let's just be content with the rest of the many kids that we have." (Our collective blood boils while our jaws hit the floor even imagining such a response!)

No one with any amount of heart or compassion would ever think this way, much less act out these thoughts. The father was absolutely correct to leave the rest of his kids and find the daughter who had wandered away. Thankfully, as he searched, he found his child . . . and he also found a new and vibrant joy.

Another family story goes like this: an older couple, celebrating their wedding anniversary, took an epic 10-day adventure throughout Europe. All of their kids were grown and independent, and encouraged Mom and Dad to finally travel as they had always desired. So, on this special occasion, they did just that. They took trains throughout the European countryside, and double decker buses in the cities; they stayed in grandiose hotels with verandas overlooking the public squares. One evening, at a romantic restaurant table outdoors beside the cobblestones, the husband gave his wife what he had given her every year of their marriage: a ring. At their proposal many years ago, he presented her with a diamond engagement ring, on their wedding day he matched it with her wedding band, and at every anniversary thereafter he surprised her with yet another ring to wear. Even though she grew expectant of it each year, the wife still adored those rings, accessorizing them with the rest of her jewelry collection that was growing now in such great number because of the many years they had been together. On this particular trip, the wife chose to bring nine other rings to match with her vacation attire—truthfully expecting one more (now ten rings total) at their anniversary dinner—so that every day of their travels she could wear a different and unique ring that her husband had given her.

As the trip neared its conclusion, and as the couple began to pack up their belongings at the hotel that final day, the wife was not able to find all ten of her husbands' gifted rings, but could only come up with nine. She was heartbroken that she had lost one. Rather than giving up hope, she began to grow in her diligence and eager searching for the missing ring. She unpacked every one of the suitcases, flinging clothes about the bedspread in search for the missing piece of cherished jewelry. She looked in every corner and crevice of the hotel room, and under every piece of furniture. Even though she was well aware that the housekeeping staff would be cleaning the hotel after their departure, she herself still swept and wiped every surface of the suite, looking for that most precious ring. Much to her relief, after a number of long hours of searching, she found the ring—and celebrated with her husband once more, like he had just gifted it to her again for the first time.

This is another heartwarming tale . . . that could just as easily be be-trayed by mathematics and logistics. Even though the wife's emotions led to the frantic search, some conventional wisdom might just as easily creep in with the rationality that she had *multitudes* of other rings not only in her suitcase, but also back at home. They had been married many years, with a ring to show it for each anniversary; surely the rest of those rings would have been sufficient enough, rather than going through the agony of wasting the day sleuthing for jewelry, unpacking luggage that was already packed and ready to return home. Further, the anniversary-celebrating husband would have instantly lost all marriage credibility if he shared the same senti-ment: "Honey, let it go. It's just a ring, for crying out loud! You've got nine more in your bag, with plenty of others at home in your jewelry armoire. Who cares about this paltry missing ring? Having nine out of ten seems like a good enough average for me." (And our respective hand-palms would all collectively smack our foreheads, bemoaning the knuckleheadedness of this dumb husband, if he were indeed to blow the entire anniversary trip with an idiotic statement such as this!)

No one with any ounce of mercy or compassion would ever think this way, much less act out these thoughts. The wife was absolutely correct to search for the missing ring, and find it to complete not only the set, but also to honor her husband's heartfelt sentiment. Thankfully, as she searched, she found the ring . . . and she also found a new and vibrant joy.

Jesus tells stories just the same—in fact, they are the ground and basis for the relational family stories that I have shared above. In Luke 15, Jesus talks about a sheep that wandered away from the flock, and a shepherd who leaves ninety-nine other sheep and finds the one who was lost. Jesus also talks about one special and sentimental coin out of ten that a woman lost, and the woman who did not rest until she was able to find the coin and com-plete not only her joy, but also her collection. Jesus then, in Luke 15:11–32, tells a very familiar story that I believe people today have egregiously mis-named: it is referred to by many as "The Parable of the Prodigal Son."

Now before anyone's feathers ruffle more than they may have from that last statement of mine, and prior to someone accusing me of blasphemy or heresy after reading my words stating that I believe one of Jesus' parables from Scripture is "misnamed," please allow for me to clarify. The original text of the Bible came to us, thousands of years ago and thousands of miles away, *from* an ancient eastern context and its languages *into* our western cul-ture and English translations (as well as whatever other language you prefer to read the same). When the canon of Scripture began to be authenticated[1]

---

1. I say that the Bible became "authenticated" because, contrary to popular belief,

by followers of Jesus Christ (and others alike), it contained simply and purely the text of the words itself. This is much differently than we have in our Bibles today. Now, that does not at all mean that Bibles in the English language (or in any other language, for that matter) in the 21st century are flawed or errant at all; that is not what I am saying either. All that I mean is that publishers of our Bibles today, and throughout history, have chosen to help us read God's Word with more organization in whatever ways they saw fit, adding in structures that they believed to be preferable.

For example: the biblical text, when inspired by God, did not originally come with chapter and verse numeration. It did not come with footnotes for clarity—such as when ancient monies or units of measure were used, and

---

that was exactly the process of the compilation of the Bible as we know it. Many people errantly believe that secret societies and councils of flawed men met in basements and caves, deciding themselves which ancient texts deserved to make it in to the Bible, and which ones were thrown out; this is an unfortunately gross misunderstanding of the collection of the biblical canon. What is more accurate is that, throughout history, people began to look collectively at many writings—some biblical and some extra-biblical (or non-biblical)—and the texts of Scripture were seen by many people over much time to *be* the *authentically* inspired Word of God. This is starkly different than people believing that councils and collections of men took all kinds of texts, on equal footing, and *called* or *decided* that some of them were Scripture, while *calling* others of them non-Scripture. That is simply not correct. What God has inspired to be written, as Scripture, does not need for man nor men to quantify or qualify it as being from God; he has already declared it to be his Word from its inspiration! The process of biblical canonization—the collection of the Bible as we know it—is indeed a self-authenticating discipline, and can be well-described by one of my former seminary professors with the following analogy: if while standing on a street corner, waiting to cross a busy intersection, you happened to hear a rumble of an engine and the deep roar of a motorcycle's throttle, you might suspect, "Hey, that sounds like a Harley-Davidson." If a minute later you saw dozens of other motorcycles that all had the same iconic sound, donned with chrome and ridden by leather vest-wearing riders, you could speak genuinely and *authentically* that they were a bunch of Harleys on an organized afternoon ride. Now you yourself, standing on that street corner, did not come up with the name of a previously unnamed motorcycle ("Harley-Davidson" in this case), in just the same way that councils of people did not gather together secretly and "name" certain writings as "The Bible" when they were previously unknown to all. Rather, you were able to simply call something as it already was—much like people throughout history could authenticate writings inspired by God as such, and others as those that were not. Back to the street corner analogy: if a few minutes after watching the Harley ride, you also heard a high-pitched buzz of a pedestrian motor-scooter being ridden by a hipster college student in a backwards ballcap with a journalist's satchel, you could clearly authenticate which things belonged together, and which were expected to remain separate. You were not a judge or officer of the law dictating which two-wheeled devices were allowed to ride together and which could not. You were simply stating that which is true as it is. So it was with the self-authentication of God's Word: it was evidenced by many, throughout centuries of history, and even within its own writings (being prophesied about and quoted within), complete as the canon of Scripture that we have today.

the footnote's clarification to our modern-day equivalent.[2] God's inspired Word did not even come with titles for the books of the Bible—many of the Bible's books were so named based upon the first words of that book,[3] or the main character, core audience, or even the divinely-inspired human author.[4] Our Bibles today have much ancillary material that was added in by current translators or publishers, such as maps, diagrams, cross-references, the formatting of the table of contents (even the table of contents itself), and not to mention the different typeset of font used. None of these things are original to the inspired, infallible, and inerrant original autographical text of God's Word. Even punctuation and spacing was not considered commonplace or preferable in some of the oldest manuscript texts![5]

Another instance of those late-additions to our modern-printed Bibles is the chapter or segment headings. Some Bibles may have them; others do not. Often, Bible translators or publishers will *italicize* the chapter headings in order to distinguish them from the original text of Scripture. If you are curious or are a person that enjoys self-discovery, then I encourage you to look up the same passage of Scripture in a few different translations of the Bible, and see if their chapter (or section) headings differ in wording a bit (or to notice if some Bible publishers have chosen to remove the headings

---

2. A wonderful example of this, from a passage of Scripture that will be brought up later in this appendix, is Luke 10:35, where the good Samaritan "took out two denarii and gave them to the innkeeper." In many Bibles, a footnote exists at the word "denarii," describing that a denarius was an ancient monetary measure equivalent to a day's wages for the common laborer. Without the 21st century English publisher or translators' addition of many footnotes like these, we would be at quite a cultural loss for some of the finer points of biblical study and readership.

3. One example is the first book of the Bible, named "Genesis" (which means "beginnings"), so named because of the first words of that book, "In the beginning . . . "

4. Examples of these are: "Ruth," anonymously written but still revolving around the central heroine of the text, that being the Moabite woman named Ruth; "Romans," named because the letter was written "to all those in Rome who are loved by God and called to be saints" (Rom 1:7); and "Matthew" (or "The Gospel According to Matthew"), which was written under the inspiration of God the Holy Spirit by Matthew the disciple of Jesus.

5. Canyouimaginetryingtoreadtextwithoutanypunctuationorspacingbetweenwords? (Still with me?) Yet that was exactly how ancient text was originally written. One of the many reasons is because of the premium of the medium on what things were written. We take paper so much for granted today that we throw it out—or recycle it at best. But before the advent of common paper, written text was either: chiseled on "steeles" (stone spires or tablets), scratched on pottery or clay, impressed on dried animal hides, or inked upon sheets of woven papyrus reads (along with a few other things). Imagine wanting to write something down, but having to wait until a cow was killed in the pasture, skinned, and the hides bleached and dried first. You would certainly not want to waste *any* space or opportunity to write because of the arduous process at that time.

altogether). Many of these non-original headings are passed down through history—much more recent history at that—and many others still are at the discretion of the publisher's editorial board for that particular printed copy of the Bible.

Now, with that clarification in view, I hope that nobody reading this appendix has any grounds to accuse me of advocating for the change of God's perfect Word. I do not desire any alteration from what God has said, and I stand firmly upon Scripture in all things. My musings about one parable of Jesus in particular (and namely the common heading that it is given, and the self-imposed title by which we remember it all the same), lead me to ponder as to whether people in the past and present have misunderstood the intention behind one of Jesus' more heartwarming and beloved stories.

I mentioned earlier in this appendix that in the first verses of Luke 15, Jesus told two stories—about a shepherd who pursued one sheep out of ninety-nine, and about a woman who searched for one lost coin out of ten. In Luke 15:11–32, Jesus shares about another family, where the father had two sons. The older son stayed wisely with the father and served faithfully in the estate. The younger son acted selfishly and foolishly, and asked for the father's inheritance that would be due to him upon the father's death. Essentially, the younger son wished the father dead, and only cared about the money that was coming to him in return. The humble father gave the younger son his request, and watched this foolish son disappear and squander his wealth. Only later on, when the son was near to starvation after having lost everything, did this son realize that humble and penitent servitude given back to his father would be better than starving to death. But when the son returned, the father didn't subjugate him to family slavery; instead, the father *restored* the son to right relationship, with utter forgiveness and grace, and realized a new level of joy because of the son's return home—with this son likely also realizing the incredibleness of reconciliation and compassionate mercy all the while.

Many people are familiar with the parable of the prodigal (or the lost) son. Many people, along with scholars and theologians, similarly refer to this parable as such, because the vast majority of the story deals with this foolish child and his flagrant behavior. However, upon looking closer at not only the text, but also the *context* prior to the text, I suggest to you that this parable ought to be renamed—or at least re-understood—with Jesus' original intent in view.

There are a number of themes in each of these stories that Jesus shares in Luke 15. The easiest to see is the idea of something being "lost." There is the lost sheep in Luke 15:4–7, the lost coin in Luke 15:8–10, and essentially the lost (or prodigal) son in Luke 15:11–32. Jesus certainly desires to share with his hearers that part of his mission on earth is "to seek and to save the lost." (Luke 19:10). In fact, when Jesus told these parables, he was doing just that: spending time with sinful people in need of a Savior, and sharing with them about the kingdom of God (as it says in Luke 15:1, "Now the tax collectors and sinners were all drawing near to hear him."). However, that is not the only audience for Jesus' stories, and that is not the only theme in these parables either.

Restored joy is another thematic thread linking all three of these stories of Jesus in Luke 15. When the shepherd found the lost sheep:

> "He calls together his friends and his neighbors, saying to them, '*Rejoice* with me, for I have found my sheep that was lost.' Just so, I tell you, there will be *more joy* in heaven over one sinner who repents" (Luke 15:6–7, emphasis mine).

Similarly, when the woman found her lost coin:

> "She calls together her friends and neighbors, saying, '*Rejoice* with me, for I have found the coin that I had lost.' Just so, I tell you, there is *joy* before the angels of God over one sinner who repents" (Luke 15:9–10, emphasis mine).

So, also, is the case when the father finds that his prodigal son has returned home, in Luke 15:20–32:

> "His father saw him and *felt compassion*, and *ran* and *embraced* him and *kissed* him. 'Bring quickly the best robe, and put it on him, and put a ring on his hand, and shoes on his feet. And bring the fattened calf and kill it, and let us eat and *celebrate*. For this my son was dead, and is alive again; he was lost, and is found.' And they began to *celebrate* . . . [the father said] '*It was fitting to celebrate and be glad*'" (emphasis mine).

One of my joys as a preacher and Bible communicator is to encourage people not only to read and know *what* the Bible says, but also *why* it has to be said. As I have mentioned before, the context behind the content is often very telling. Luke 15 is not one to disappoint in the least, for the context of these three stories is as follows, in verses 2–3:

> " . . . And the Pharisees and the scribes *grumbled*, saying, 'This man *receives sinners* and eats with them.' *So he told them this parable*" (emphasis mine).

The grumbling of those in Jesus' periphery, who likewise heard Jesus' parables, was not only an additional part of the stories; it is the most integral piece coming from the direct audience of those tales. Further, the "So" that begins verse 3 in this text of Luke 15 is a bit of justification for exactly *why* Jesus told the stories in the first place—almost as if "*because* of the grumbling of those around Jesus, *he told these specific stories.*" Additionally, since there is absolutely no break between the triad parables of the lost sheep, lost coin, and lost (prodigal) son, it is easy and appropriate to group them all as one broader story, akin to the singular "this parable" at the end of verse 3. Jesus cracks open the trilogy, for the purpose of giving a lesson to these grumbling Pharisees and scribes and compassionless Savior-haters.

And that is why I believe the "Parable of the Prodigal Son" is misnamed.

I see the context being remarkably clear as to the reason and intent that Jesus shared this story: it was to rebuke and correct the gruff mercilessness of not only those who followed Jesus on the fringe, but those who specifically *should have been* the guides and the givers of God's mercy and compassion to the sinful community in need of it in the first place. The Pharisees and scribes were to be experts of the Word of God, but they showed instead that they became oblivious to the intention of it.[6] For this reason, Jesus told them three stories to describe them—or to contrast them with whom they ought to be.

The parable of the lost sheep shows that Jesus' doubters ought to be joyful that he is seeking those who need to be restored to the flock.[7] After all, "sinners" are truly the ones who need to be found in the first place, as opposed to the "ninety-nine righteous persons who need no repentance" (Luke 15:7). The parable of the lost coin, additionally, reiterates the joy that *should* be had by the surrounding community, when sinners actually come to Jesus (as opposed to the grumbling that the Pharisees and others had when sinners came to him in their presence).

And then that next parable . . . well . . . I suggest that it should be renamed based on its conclusion—which most people forget about, or have never fully read. We see the end of this great parable in Luke 15:24–32. After the reconciliation between the father and the younger son:

---

6. See, for example, Matt 9:9–13, and Matt 12:1–8. In these two places, the crowds around Jesus were much the same as in Luke 15 ("many tax collectors and sinners") and in Matt 9:10, along with these common opponents, the Pharisees. On two different occasions, Jesus compelled their supposed knowledge of the Word of God—even quoting it in Hos 6:6—and showed them that the purpose of God's Word is to bring people, compassionately, to a restored relationship with God through himself, Jesus Christ. Instead, these fringe contrarians, the Pharisees, were regularly satisfied to bitterly distance people from their restoration to God.

7. See, as well, Matt 10:6 and Matt 15:24, where Jesus declares that he was sent "to the lost sheep of the house of Israel."

"[The father said] 'For this my son [the prodigal] was dead, and
is alive again; he was lost, and is found.' And they began to celebrate. Now his *older son* was in the field, and as he came and
drew near to the house, he heard music and dancing. And he
called one of the servants and asked what these things meant.
And he said to him, 'Your brother has come, and your father has
killed the fattened calf, because he has received him back safe
and sound.' *But he was angry* and refused to go in. His father
came out and entreated him, but he answered his father, 'Look,
these many years I have served you, and I never disobeyed your
command, yet you never gave me a young goat, that I might
celebrate with my friends. But when this son of yours came, who
has devoured your property with prostitutes,[8] you killed the fattened calf for him!' And he said to him, 'Son, you are always
with me, and all that is mine is yours. *It was fitting to celebrate
and be glad*, for this your brother was dead, and is alive; he was
lost, and is found'" (emphasis mine).

The secret is out: I prefer to call this story "The Parable of the *Non-
Prodigal Son*." Jesus is telling a tale for this specific intent: that his opponents would be so named in the story, and realize that their disgruntled
attitudes and preference for irreconciliation must be waylaid and exchanged
for joy and compassion in the repentant kingdom of God. When looking at
the contextual reason as to *why* Jesus shared this parable in the first place,
we can be more aware as to not only what the central thrust of the parable is
about, but also what it might be better named in order to help others grasp
its intent.

Another example of looking at the "why a parable was spoken or
written" that can help us understand God's intention for our lives, and our
responsibility in healthy relationships, is in another epic parable of Jesus in
Luke 10:30–37. Here, in the "Parable of the Good Samaritan" (which I am
fine with being so named, by the way), we read about a man falling on the
down-and-out. He was robbed, beaten, stripped, and left for dead. Two religious people happened to be passing by the man—one at a time ("a priest"
first, then "a Levite" next). It might seem as if these men, above all others,
would have stopped to help the poor guy out. However, in Jesus' story, these
men passed by without doing a thing. It took a third man, someone whose
ethnic and cultural background made him loathed in the community (and

8. I see this as Jesus' subtle reference to what the Pharisees and scribes thought of
" . . . the tax collectors and sinners" in Jesus' presence. According to these ungrateful
and unmerciful Pharisees, I suspect that they most assuredly saw those who squander
their money and morality with prostitutes as the same descriptive designation of the
rabble who hung around Jesus searching for their salvation.

this can be seen by the contrasting verbiage, "but a Samaritan"), and it was he who finally came to the injured man's aid to restore him to life.

Once again, just like the aforementioned "Parable of the (Non)-Prodigal Son," many people also do not read or know the context (or the ending) of the "Parable of the Good Samaritan." This story from Jesus begins and ends as follows:

> "And behold, a lawyer stood up to put him to the test, saying, 'Teacher, what shall I do to inherit eternal life?' He said to him, 'What is written in the Law? How do you read it?' And he answered, 'You shall love the Lord your God with all your heart and with all your soul and with all your strength and with all your mind, and your neighbor as yourself.' And he said to him, 'You have answered correctly; do this, and you will live.' *But he [the lawyer], desiring to justify himself,* said to Jesus, 'And who is my neighbor?' Jesus replied . . . [after telling the parable of the good Samaritan] 'Which of these three, do you think, proved to be a neighbor to the man who fell among the robbers?' He said, 'The one who showed him mercy.' And Jesus said to him, *'You go, and do likewise'*" (Luke 10:25-30a, 36-37, emphasis mine).

I was recently in a conversation with someone who quoted the parable of the "Good Samaritan," and brought it up asking me the question, "So, Pastor, who do *you* think is your neighbor?" I answered akin to what I believe Jesus was teaching, saying "Well, my neighbor is whomever is in need of compassion and mercy; in other words, everyone around me is my neighbor." However, the person who was speaking with me disagreed, and brought up other details of Jesus' good Samaritan story, sharing that the Samaritan was considered a good neighbor while the priest and Levite were not rebuked and were somehow left off the hook. He concluded his sentiment by saying, "See, in Jesus' story, even Jesus showed that not everyone needs to be a neighbor after all (for the priest and the Levite were not considered neighbors in the parable, but only the Samaritan was)." This person speaking with me was trying to justify not being neighborly, because Jesus did not explicitly condemn the priest nor the Levite for their own preferences.

After hearing this in conversation, my squirm became so palpable that I almost fell off my chair.

This person in conversation with me was an illustration *par excellence* of laying their presuppositions on top of God's Word (which was brought up in chapter 5, "Relationship Objections"), as well as the necessity mentioned earlier in this appendix to understand the intention as to why Jesus tells his parables before coming to our own conclusions. Jesus did not share about the good Samaritan in order to give us justification to be like the priest and Levite, nor to say that because the priest and Levite were *not* neighbors to the wounded man that we are somehow similarly justified to recognize that not everyone around us is our neighbor (or that it's okay to not be neighborly with others). This is in fact the exact opposite of Jesus' intention in telling the parable! The beginning of this parable had a man—someone who was expertly precise in justifying himself in the eyes of the law (akin to "a lawyer" in Luke 10:25)—who was trying to get Jesus' go-ahead in treating other people badly. The man was "desiring to justify himself" (verse 29) and use Jesus as his proof. And it was precisely for this very reason that Jesus told him the parable of the good Samaritan.[9]

Jesus wanted to challenge the man's self-justification and preferential norms by precisely saying "Anyone—indeed *everyone*—who is in need of mercy is to be considered your neighbor, for you to show compassionate mercy to them." The rest of the details of the parable are only dressing for the gravity of the story—the punch-line, if you will—and are not to be read into as explanations or justifications for other things outside of the purpose and intention that Jesus gave the overall parable in the first place. Said another way with a common idiom, "we must not lose the forest through the trees."

One of my Irish extended family members tells a joke about an Englishman, a Scotsman, and an Irishman who all were running from the police. Wanting to flee from the paddywaggon, they found their way onto an empty railyard and inside an abandoned boxcar. There inside were three burlap sacks, so each one jumped inside a sack to hide. When the police arrived, they noticed the three stuffed and rumpled sacks, so the officer nudged the one bag with his foot and the hidden Englishman inside responded, "Woof, woof!" The officer thought to himself, "Ah, must be dogs in the sack." Moving on to the second bag, which he nudged, the hiding Scotsman responded, "Meow, meow!" The officer thought again, "Ah, must be cats in the sack." Now on to the third bag, the officer nudged it and inside the Irishman responded, "Sack o' potatoes, sack o' potatoes!"

It should be clear that the reason for such a joke—once again, told by one of my endearing Dublin-born extended family members, so I feel

9. Notice that Jesus does not have the hero in the parable be "a lawyer," and we do not call this parable "The Parable of the Good Lawyer." Precisely the opposite: Samaritans were lowly and despised people in the ancient Jewish culture, so an expert in the Jewish law would have loathed the fact that Jesus made the hero a Samaritan man. In fact, there are textual clues that the lawyer, realizing this fact, could not even bear himself to say the word "Samaritan" in reply to Jesus, for when Jesus asks him who was neighborly, the lawyer did not reply "Well, surely Jesus, it was the Samaritan man"; instead, the man could only barely muster, "The one who showed him mercy" (Luke 10:37).

justified to share it—is to rib the ironic innocence and humor of his fun-loving Irish heritage. Now if someone heard this joke told at a house party and replied with "That's right, and that's exactly why I don't trust the Scottish and certainly no Brits either, for they are the wildest lying thieves the world has ever seen," then the person touting that interpretation of the joke ought to be tossed in a burlap sack themselves! The purpose of the humorous story is to get to the punchline—to cause a room full of people to smile and laugh on behalf of the silly Irishman. The Englishman and the Scotsman are simply complementary characters, never meant to receive a nod or academy award for supporting actor. It is true that they are not irrelevant in the tale, for the joke makes a bit more sense given that they all are geographical compatriots within the British Isles. However, the lesson of that story is to hang on the reality of the punchline.

Jesus' parables are not jokes, to be sure. But they do have significance in their reality, and in the main intention or big idea of the story. In the illustrations and stories that Jesus the Son of God shares with us, the greatest take-away from those parables and teachings is for us to understand the primary purpose as to why they are told. "The Parable of the Good Samaritan" is told so that *anyone* "who [needs to be shown] mercy" (Luke 10:37a) would receive mercy; indeed, that we would "go and do likewise'" (verse 37b) to all in the world. Jesus did not tell that parable as a mathematical treatise regarding whether or not there are others around us or different than us who are not our neighbors, and if we are justified to treat them un-neighborly as a result. No, Jesus says to love, forgive, and show compassionate mercy, regardless of whether they are seen as friends or enemies alike. Similarly, "The Parable of the (Non)-Prodigal Son" is told so that we would similarly see that our hearts are to be filled with joy in showing mercy to others—even and especially those different and seemingly undeserving from us. In that way, we would be cautious seeing ourselves as the "grumbl[ing]" spectators of repentance and reconciliation (Luke 15:2). No, Jesus says we are to "rejoice" and "celebrate" at restoration (Luke 15:6, 9, 24), hearing the truth that "it was fitting to celebrate and be glad" (verse 32).

Jesus' teaching is never contradictory, and is always complementary, and the oft-misnamed prodigal parable gives testimony to this fact. God desires for lost people to come to saving faith in Jesus Christ, in order to experience a right relationship with him. God also desires compassion and joy within restoration, both in our relationship to God and in our relationships with others. The rules of reconciliation in God's kingdom are no different vertically (between us and God) than they are horizontally (between us and others). In fact, this precise kind of hypocrisy is what distanced the lawyers and Pharisees and scribes and others from truly knowing God and properly interpreting his Scriptures.

There are some distinctions with regards to God's calls and commands for us, to be sure—namely, that being nice is not our sole and exclusive command (as one cannot receive heaven simply by being nice to everyone on earth). Rather, precisely because we were lost and now found, and precisely because we have been shown forgiveness and reconciliation and grace for eternity, we can have joy in God because of Jesus Christ. As a result of that vertical joy, we are called to not "grumble" but rather are expected to give grace and have compassion on others because God showed his grace and compassion to us. The truth is that we are found in Jesus' parable, no matter where we are and no matter how we act. We must be grateful to God to be called a former prodigal, and especially careful to *not* be associated as the non-prodigal son.

Appendix II

Stay In Touch

SHARE YOUR RELATIONSHIP JOYS and seek encouragement through your relation*s*lip struggles.

Follow us on:

Twitter: @relationslipsBK

Instagram: @relationslipsbk

E-mail: relationslipsBOOK@mail.com

Bibliography

Begg, Alistair. *Forgiving and Forgiven, Part One*. Truth for Life Audio, 9 April 2000. https://www.truthforlife.org/resources/sermon/forgiven-forgiving-pt-1/.

———. "No Retaliation!" Sermon, Chagrin Falls, OH, Parkside Church, March 27, 2011.

Crabb, Larry. *Connecting*. Nashville: W. Publishing Group, 1997.

———. *The Safest Place on Earth*. Nashville: W. Publishing Group, 1999.

Drapeau, Jason. "Relationships *not* Relationships: Life Together Based on Jesus' Words in Luke 6:27–49." *Africanus Journal*, Vol. 11 No. 1 (April 2019), 5–12. http://wincc. org/leadership-team/pastor-jason-drapeau/africanus-journal-vol-11-no1.pdf.

Grinberg, Emanuella. "A former UK officer was convicted of rape on a Tinder date, but his victim says trauma is a 'life sentence.'" *CNN*, July 14, 2019. https://www.cnn. com/2019/07/13/us/antigua-rape-trial-extradition/index.html.

Herklots, Rosamond. "Forgive Our Sins as We Forgive." In *Amazing Grace: Hymn Texts for Devotional Use*. Edited by Bertus Frederick Polman, Marilyn Kay Stulken, James Rawlings Syndor. Louisville: Westminster John Knox, 1994.

Lewis, C. S. *The Weight of Glory*. New York: Harper Collins, 1949, 2001. http://www. desiringgod.org/blog/posts/c-s-lewis-on-the-problem-of-forgiveness.

Menninger, Karl, Martin Mayman, and Paul Pruyser. *The Vital Balance*. New York: Viking, 1963.

Nietzsche, Friedrich Wilhelm. *The Gay Science: or The Joyful Wisdom*. Translated by Thomas Common. Whithorn, Scotland: Anodos, 1910, 2019.

Payne, Tony. *How to Walk into Church*. Youngstown: Matthias Media, 2015.

Piper, John. "Prayer: The Work of Missions." *A.C.M.C. Annual Meeting*. Denver: July 29, 1988. https://www.desiringgod.org/messages/prayer-the-work-of-missions.

Plummer, Alfred. *An Exegetical Commentary on the Gospel According to St. Matthew*. New York: Charles Scribner's Sons, 1910.

Smedes, Lewis B. *Forgive and Forget: Healing the Hurts We Don't Deserve*. San Francisco: Harper Collins, 1996.

www.ingramcontent.com/pod-product-compliance
Lightning Source LLC
Chambersburg PA
CBHW060413090426
42734CB00011B/2297